one million things

SPACE

**LONDON, NEW YORK,
MELBOURNE, MUNICH, AND DELHI**

For Tall Tree Ltd.:
Editors Neil Kelly, Claudia Martin, and Jon Richards
Designers Ben Ruocco and Ed Simkins

For Dorling Kindersley:
Senior editor Carron Brown
Senior designer Philip Letsu

Managing editor Linda Esposito
Managing art editor Diane Thistlethwaite

Commissioned photography Stefan Podhorodecki
Creative retouching Steve Willis

Publishing manager Andrew Macintyre
Category publisher Laura Buller

DK picture researcher Myriam Megharbi
Production editor Marc Staples
Production controller Charlotte Oliver

Jacket design Hazel Martin
Jacket editor Matilda Gollon
Design development manager Sophia M. Tampakopoulos Turner
Development team Yumiko Tahata

First published in the United States in 2010 by
DK Publishing,
375 Hudson Street, New York, New York 10014

A catalog catalogue record for this book
is available from the Library of Congress

ISBN: 978-0-75666-289-9

Printed and bound by Leo, China

**Discover more at
www.dk.com**

one million things

SPACE

Written by:
Carole Stott
Consultant:
Jacqueline Mitton

1

Universe

2

Stars

3

The solar system

4

Exploration

5

Space travelers

Contents

GALAXIES GALORE
The universe is populated by galaxies—huge collections of stars. The galaxies shown here belong to a group of five known as Stephan's Quintet. The bright stars in view are closer and belong to the Milky Way Galaxy.

Universe

BIG BANG

The universe started in an event known as the Big Bang, which occurred about 13.7 billion years ago. It was a type of explosion that produced everything in today's universe—all energy, matter, and space—and marked the start of time. Back then, the universe looked nothing like it does today, but everything that exists now existed in some form then. Although the amount of material and energy the universe is made of has remained the same, it has been cooling, expanding, and changing ever since it came into being.

❶ AT THE START

No one knows what came before the Big Bang, or why it occurred, but we have put together the story since almost the instant of the universe's creation. The universe was created in a tiny fraction of a second. It was then an exceptionally hot and an immensely dense ball of radiation energy. It was also microscopically small, but within a trillionth of a second it ballooned to about the size of a soccer pitch, before settling down to a slower rate of expansion.

❷ HOT STUFF

The very young universe was incredibly hot, about 1,800 trillion trillion °F (1,000 trillion trillion °C). Within one-thousandth of a second, its tiny radiation particles produced tiny particles of matter. Within three minutes the Universe was an opaque "foggy soup" of particles, which were mainly hydrogen and helium nuclei. The universe stayed this way for 300,000 years, expanding and cooling to 4,900°F (2,700°C).

❸ FIRST ATOMS

The first atoms formed when the universe was 300,000 years old. Hydrogen and helium nuclei joined with protons and electrons, which are other tiny particles, to make atoms. This ordinary matter consisted of 76 percent hydrogen and 24 percent helium, with a trace of lithium. The hydrogen and helium would go on to produce all the elements found in today's universe.

Atomic nuclei

Helium atom

Hydrogen atom

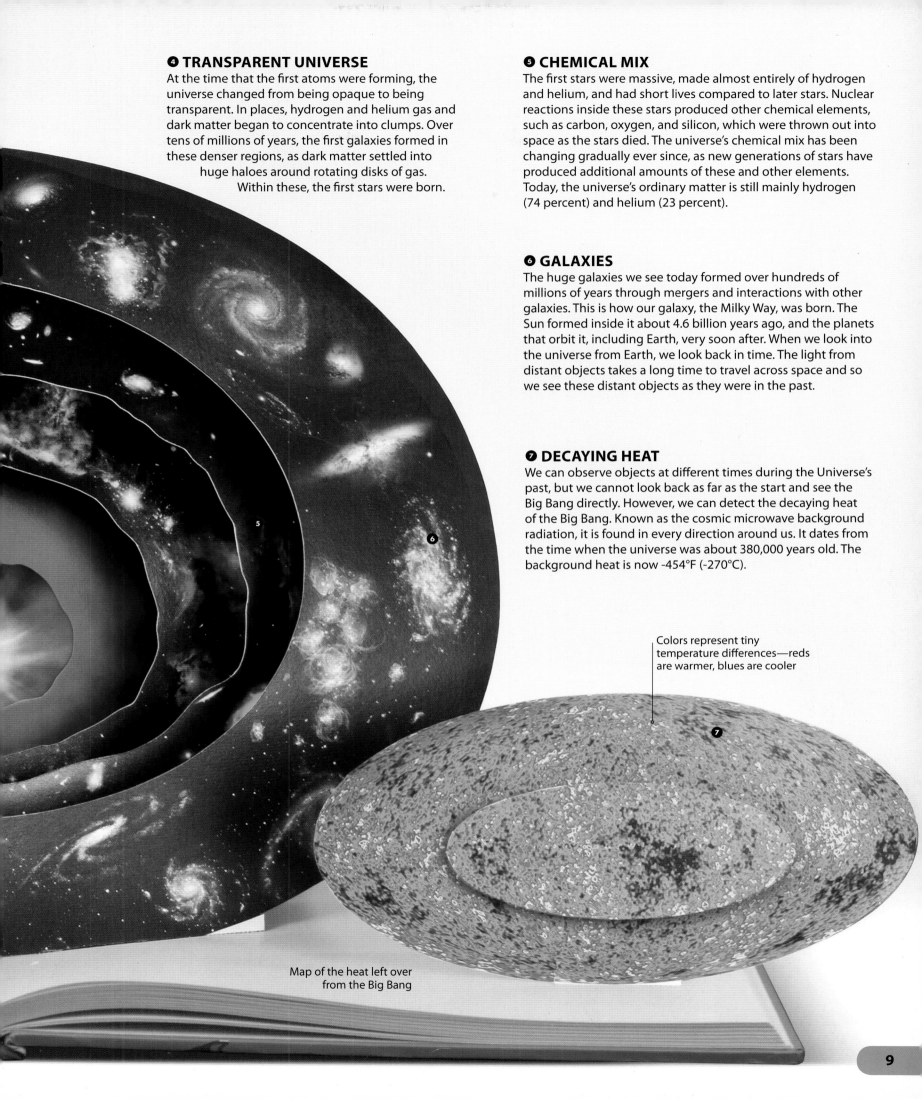

❹ TRANSPARENT UNIVERSE

At the time that the first atoms were forming, the universe changed from being opaque to being transparent. In places, hydrogen and helium gas and dark matter began to concentrate into clumps. Over tens of millions of years, the first galaxies formed in these denser regions, as dark matter settled into huge haloes around rotating disks of gas. Within these, the first stars were born.

❺ CHEMICAL MIX

The first stars were massive, made almost entirely of hydrogen and helium, and had short lives compared to later stars. Nuclear reactions inside these stars produced other chemical elements, such as carbon, oxygen, and silicon, which were thrown out into space as the stars died. The universe's chemical mix has been changing gradually ever since, as new generations of stars have produced additional amounts of these and other elements. Today, the universe's ordinary matter is still mainly hydrogen (74 percent) and helium (23 percent).

❻ GALAXIES

The huge galaxies we see today formed over hundreds of millions of years through mergers and interactions with other galaxies. This is how our galaxy, the Milky Way, was born. The Sun formed inside it about 4.6 billion years ago, and the planets that orbit it, including Earth, very soon after. When we look into the universe from Earth, we look back in time. The light from distant objects takes a long time to travel across space and so we see these distant objects as they were in the past.

❼ DECAYING HEAT

We can observe objects at different times during the Universe's past, but we cannot look back as far as the start and see the Big Bang directly. However, we can detect the decaying heat of the Big Bang. Known as the cosmic microwave background radiation, it is found in every direction around us. It dates from the time when the universe was about 380,000 years old. The background heat is now -454°F (-270°C).

Colors represent tiny temperature differences—reds are warmer, blues are cooler

Map of the heat left over from the Big Bang

TODAY'S UNIVERSE

The universe is everything we know about, as well as everything we have yet to discover. It includes all space and time as well as everything we see or detect in other ways. Parts of the universe, such as the planets, stars, and galaxies, are familiar to us, but only make up a small amount of it. The vast majority of the universe remains unknown.

❶ ENERGETIC UNIVERSE

We learn about the universe by collecting and analyzing the energy from its objects. One form of energy is light, and this allows us to see objects. We also gain knowledge from other forms, such as X-rays. Here, an X-ray view of two galaxies reveals a jet of material powering out from around a supermassive black hole.

❷ DISTANT QUASAR

Telescopes on Earth and in space are used to collect and record information. Telescopic cameras are also on board robotic spacecraft that are sent into space. The brightest starlike object in this image by the Hubble Space Telescope is a quasar—a type of galaxy and one of the universe's most distant objects.

❸ GALAXY GROUP

The billions of galaxies in the universe are enormous collections of stars. Galaxies exist in groups and often interact with their neighbors. The Seyfert's Sextet appears to contain six galaxies, but is actually a group of just four galaxies. The object at lower right is a part of one of the galaxies, and the small spiral in the center is more distant than the other galaxies.

❹ STAR CLUSTER

There are trillions of stars in the universe. Our Sun is one—it is a huge spinning globe of hot gas and, like other stars, it follows a life cycle. Stars form in clusters within huge clouds of gas and dust. The 80 or so stars in this Butterfly Cluster were born about 100 million years ago.

❺ STAR BIRTH

In addition to stars, galaxies contain massive, cold clouds of mainly hydrogen gas. Stars are forming all the time within these clouds as fragments of the cloud condense. In this false-color infrared view of the Eagle Nebula, the stars appear blue, the gas is green, and red shows where there is dust.

❻ PLANET

One of Earth's nearest space neighbors is Mars. Along with Earth, it is one of the eight major planets that orbit the Sun. The scientific rules we live by on Earth, such as gravity, apply on Mars and all over the universe. Chemical elements found on Earth, such as oxygen, occur throughout the universe—they exist in different states depending on temperature and pressure.

❼ SMALL WORLD

Huge numbers of small bodies exist in the region of space around the Sun. They include planetary moons, such as Mimas, which is 256 miles (418 km) across and orbits Saturn. Smaller still and more numerous are the asteroids that are located between Mars and Jupiter, and the comets that are more distant from the Sun than Neptune.

Mimus's largest crater is 88 miles (140 km) wide

❽ UNKOWN UNIVERSE

The planets, stars, and galaxies are made of atoms and amount to 4.6 percent of the universe. The rest is not detected directly, but we know it is there by its effect on objects close by. It consists of dark matter and an unknown form of energy, called dark energy.

Atoms
4.6 percent

Dark matter
23 percent

Dark energy
72 percent

This star is in the foreground of the image and belongs to the Milky Way Galaxy

Some galaxies are distorted as they interact with each other

Some galaxies appear red because they are enshrouded in dust

The smallest and reddest galaxies are the most distant—they formed when the universe was about 800 million years old

This galaxy is one of about 10,000 shown in this image

DEEP SPACE

The universe is full of galaxies. They are scattered all around us and we find them no matter how deep we peer into space. The deeper and more distant we look, the farther back in time we go. The galaxies are at such huge distances that it takes millions or even billions of years for their light to reach us. We see them as they were when their light left them millions or billions of years ago. The galaxies are not randomly scattered through space but exist in groupings known as clusters. These clusters also form larger groups called superclusters, which contain thousands of galaxies.

❶ ULTRADEEP SPACE

The Hubble Space Telescope has looked into ultradeep space to give us our deepest view of the universe so far. The telescope studied a tiny patch of Earth's sky between September 2003 and January 2004 as it made 400 orbits of Earth. The view it captured shows thousands of galaxies in various sizes and shapes. There are spiral galaxies and ellipticals, as well as other peculiar shapes. The most distant galaxies are about 13 billion light years away. These are some of the youngest galaxies in the early universe. To produce the image, Hubble's camera took 800 exposures lasting about 21 minutes each—a total of 11.3 days. To look at the entire sky in this detail would take Hubble one million years of uninterrupted work.

❷ LARGE-SCALE STRUCTURE

Astronomers use computers to simulate what the large-scale structure of the universe is like. This view shows a portion of a cube-shaped region of space. The region measures approximately two billion light-years across and is populated by 20 million or so galaxies. The galaxies are distributed in a huge weblike network of chains and sheets; these are the largest structures in the universe. The chains and sheets consist of galaxy superclusters and these are separated by huge voids of virtually empty space. The superclusters are groupings of galaxy clusters, which in turn are collections of galaxies. Our Milky Way Galaxy is part of a cluster known as the Local Group. The Local Group is joined together with other clusters to form the Local Supercluster.

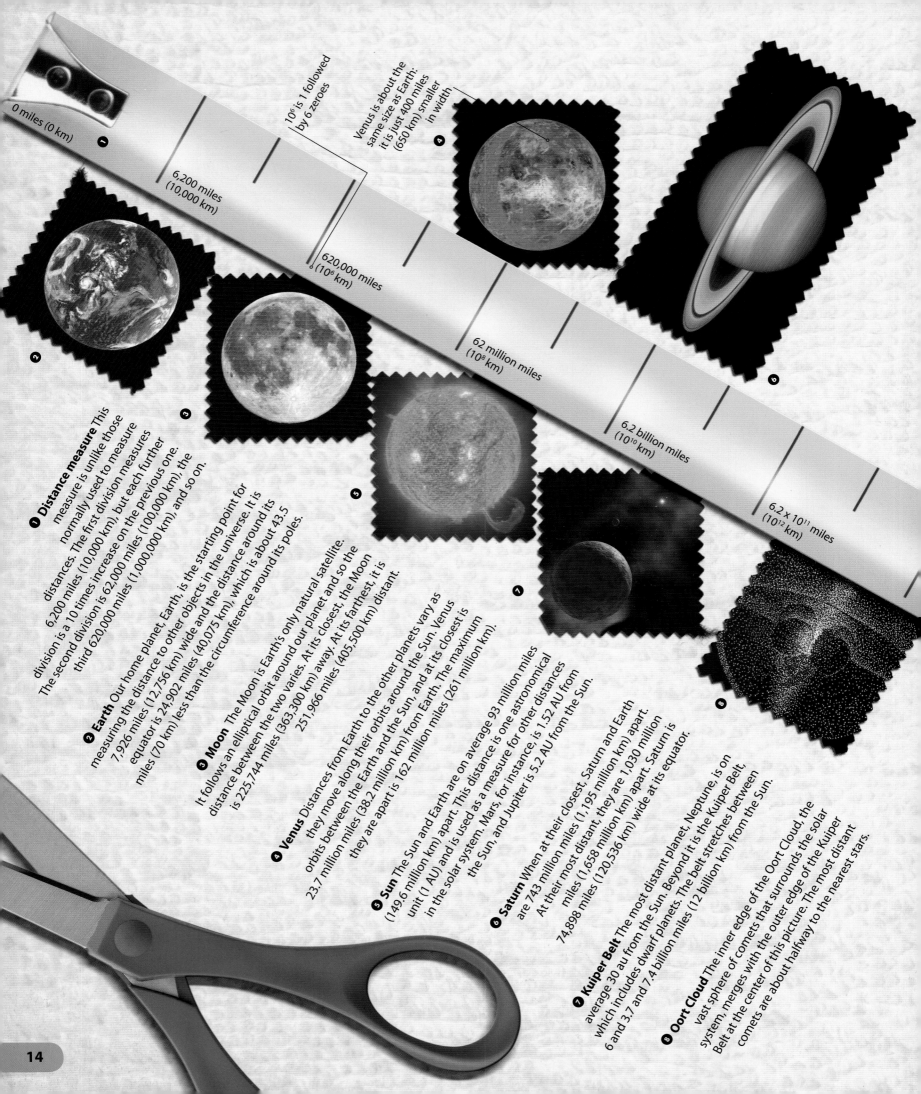

0 miles (0 km)

10^6 is 1 followed by 6 zeroes

Venus is about the same size as Earth: it is just 400 miles (650 km) smaller in width

6,200 miles (10,000 km)

620,000 miles (10^6 km)

62 million miles (10^8 km)

6.2 billion miles (10^{10} km)

6.2 x 10^{11} miles (10^{12} km)

1 Distance measure This measure is unlike those normally used to measure distances. The first division measures 6,200 miles (10,000 km), but each further division is a 10 times increase on the previous one. The second division measures 62,000 miles (100,000 km), the third 620,000 miles (1,000,000 km), and so on.

2 Earth Our home planet, Earth, is the starting point for measuring the distance to other objects in the universe. It is 7,926 miles (12,756 km) wide and the distance around its equator is 24,902 miles (40,075 km), which is about 43.5 miles (70 km) less than the circumference around its poles.

3 Moon The Moon is Earth's only natural satellite. It follows an elliptical orbit around our planet and so the distance between the two varies. At its closest, the Moon is 225,744 miles (363,300 km) away. At its farthest, it is 251,966 miles (405,500 km) distant.

4 Venus Distances from Earth to the other planets vary as they move along their orbits around the Sun. Venus orbits between the Earth and the Sun, and at its closest is 23.7 million miles (38.2 million km) from Earth. The maximum they are apart is 162 million miles (261 million km).

5 Sun The Sun and Earth are on average 93 million miles (149.6 million km) apart. This distance is one astronomical unit (1 AU) and is used as a measure for other distances in the solar system. Mars, for instance, is 1.52 AU from the Sun, and Jupiter is 5.2 AU from the Sun.

6 Saturn When at their closest, Saturn and Earth are 743 million miles (1,195 million km) apart. At their most distant, they are 1,030 million miles (1,658 million km) apart. Saturn is 74,898 miles (120,536 km) wide at its equator.

7 Kuiper Belt The most distant planet, Neptune, is on average 30 au from the Sun. Beyond it is the Kuiper Belt, which includes dwarf planets. The belt stretches between 6 and 3.7 and 7.4 billion miles (12 billion km) from the Sun.

8 Oort Cloud The inner edge of the Oort Cloud, the vast sphere of comets that surrounds the solar system, merges with the outer edge of the Kuiper Belt at the center of this picture. The most distant comets are about halfway to the nearest stars.

SCALE OF THE UNIVERSE

The universe is so vast that it is difficult to imagine how big it is. The measuring units used on Earth are inadequate, not only to measure the size of the universe, but also the distances between objects in it. Miles and kilometres are used within the solar system, but are ineffective for distances beyond it. Light-years are used instead. A single light-year is the distance that light travels in one year and this is 5.88 million million miles (9.46 million million kilometres).

9 Proxima Centauri The closest star to Earth after the Sun is Proxima Centauri. It is part of a triple star system that includes Alpha Centauri, which itself consists of two stars. Proxima Centauri is the closest of the three stars to us and it is 4.2 light-years away.

10 Milky Way The Sun is within the Milky Way Galaxy, which measures 100,000 light-years across. The Earth is positioned about 27,000 light-years from its center. The 25 next closest stars to us are all within about 12 light-years of the Sun.

11 Andromeda Galaxy The closest major galaxy to us is the Andromeda Galaxy, which is 2.5 million light years away. Although its light is moving towards us at 186,282 miles (299,792 km) per second, it is so far away that we see it as it was when the light left it 2.5 million years ago.

12 Virgo Cluster The Milky Way and about 40 other galaxies make a cluster of galaxies known as the Local Group. They occupy a volume of space more than 10 million light-years across. The center of the next nearest large cluster, the Virgo Cluster, is about 52 million light-years away.

13 Distant galaxies The most distant galaxies we can see are very young galaxies producing stars at a furious rate. In the past decade, we have observed hundreds of them as they were only a few hundred million years after the start of the universe.

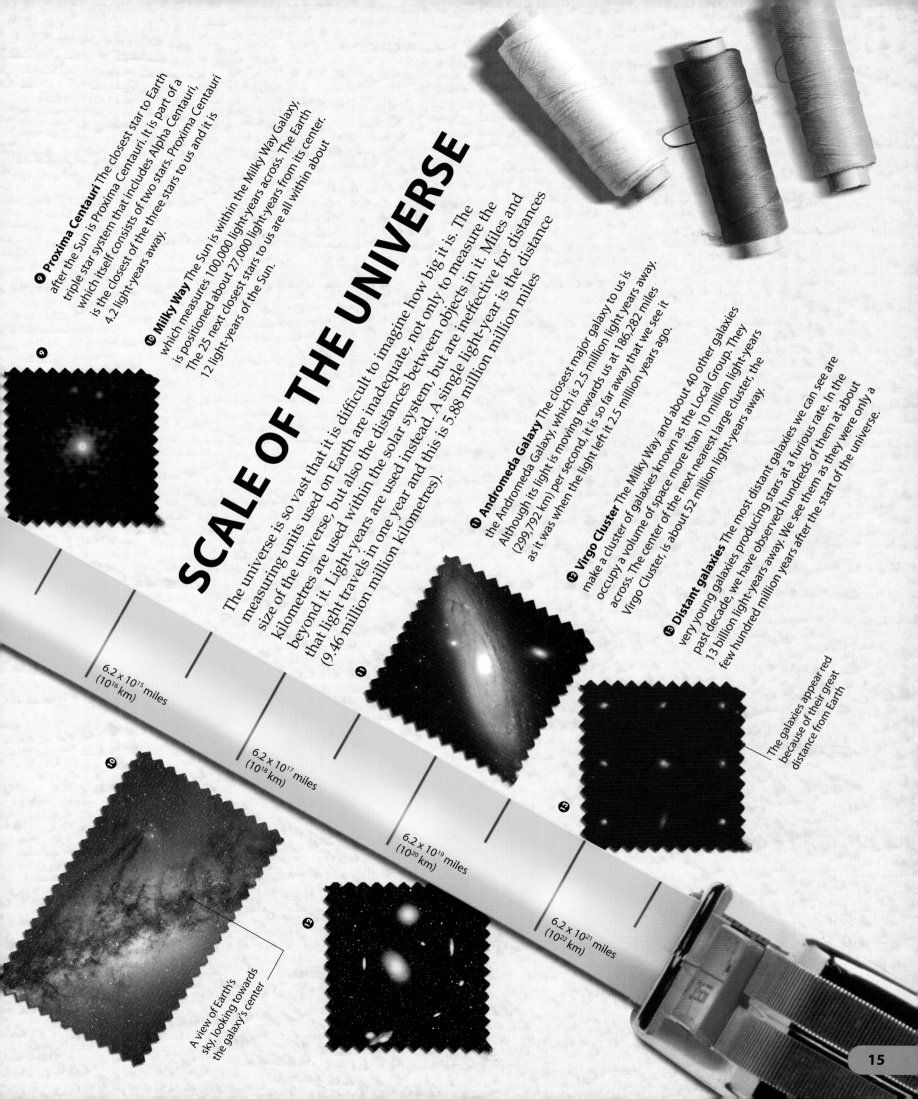

6.2 x 10^15 miles
(10^16 km)

6.2 x 10^17 miles
(10^18 km)

6.2 x 10^19 miles
(10^20 km)

6.2 x 10^21 miles
(10^22 km)

The galaxies appear red because of their great distance from Earth

A view of Earth's sky, looking towards the galaxy's center

GALAXIES

There are at least 125 billion galaxies in the universe. Each consists of a huge number of stars, vast amounts of gas and dust, and dark matter, all bound together by gravity. Galaxies come in four main shapes and in a range of sizes. Dwarf galaxies measure a few thousand light-years across and have about 10 million stars, while a giant galaxy is typically 300,000 light-years wide with 1,000 billion stars. The very center of a galaxy is known as its nucleus or core, and most galaxies, if not all, have a supermassive black hole lying there.

❶ ELLIPTICAL

Elliptical galaxies come in a range of ball shapes, from almost spherical to flattened oval. They appear smooth and featureless, and they consist of older stars. The galaxies contain little gas and dust, and have limited star formation. The majority of an elliptical galaxy's stars are on highly eccentric orbits that take them into and then out from the central region. These galaxies come in a range of sizes. M87 is one of the largest.

❷ IRREGULAR

About a quarter of all galaxies are classified as irregulars, because they have no regular shape or form. They are small and contain considerable amounts of gas and dust. In the past, they were spiral-shaped, but because they passed too close to, or even through, another galaxy, they have been pulled out of shape. Close encounters trigger star formation, so irregulars have high proportions of new and young stars. M82, the Cigar Galaxy, is irregular due to its interaction with M81, a neighboring spiral galaxy.

M87 is a giant elliptical galaxy some 120,000 light-years across and 55 million light-years away

This image of M82, in infrared wavelengths, shows dust particles (red) blown out by the galaxy's hot stars (blue)

❸ SPIRAL

Spiral galaxies consist of a bright, central bulge of stars surrounded by a flat disk of stars, gas, and dust. Spiral arms seem to wind out from the bulge. In fact, stars also exist between the arms. The spiral arms are seen clearly because they are denser regions where stars are forming and so contain many young, bright stars. The disk and bulge are surrounded by a faint halo of old stars, many of which are clumped together in globular clusters.

❹ BARRED SPIRAL

Nearly two-thirds of spiral galaxies have a barlike region of stars in their central section, and so are classified as barred spirals. Their spiral arms appear to wind out from the two ends of the bar, which is thought to channel gas and dust inwards towards the central bulge. The flow of this matter causes many barred spirals to have active nuclei, as the material fuels a central black hole. New stars also form from the gas and dust in the galaxies.

❺ SOMBRERO GALAXY

The spiral galaxy M104 is seen edge-on from Earth. It is also known as the Sombrero Galaxy, because of its passing resemblance to the Mexican hat. Its dark dust lane forms the hat's rim, and the galaxy's bulging core makes the hat's crown.

The Sombrero Galaxy is surrounded by a roughly spherical halo of about 2,000 globular clusters

The Pinwheel Galaxy, M101, is face-on to Earth. It is about twice the width of the Milky Way Galaxy and one of the largest spirals known

Like other barred spiral galaxies with large bars, NGC 1300 has a spiral structure within its bar where gas is being funneled inward

▼ BLACK EYE

A dark lane of dust in front of this spiral galaxy's bright core gives it its name—the Black Eye. The galaxy looks like a normal spiral, but is the result of a collision between two galaxies. The stars in a galaxy usually rotate in the same direction. In the Black Eye, interstellar gas in its outer region rotates in the opposite direction from the stars and gas in the inner region. This is a result of the Black Eye absorbing a smaller galaxy, perhaps more than one billion years ago.

CARTWHEEL ▼

Most galactic collisions are sideways mergers, but the Cartwheel Galaxy is the result of a head-on collision. The Cartwheel was once a normal spiral galaxy. We see it now after a smaller galaxy has moved through its core. A shockwave caused by this collision traveled out to the edge of the disturbed spiral and created a ring of energetic star formation. The smaller galaxy has moved off and is now many light years away from the collision scene.

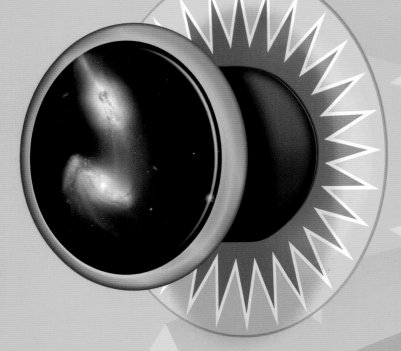

▲ MICE

These two galaxies, each with a narrow tail coming out of its long, white body, are known as the Mice. They are the result of a close encounter between two spiral galaxies some 160 million years ago. The tails are the remains of spiral arms. A stream of material links the two galaxies and they will eventually merge to form a large, ball-shaped galaxy that will be classified as an elliptical.

▼ ARP 272

The two spiral galaxies NGC 6050 and IC 1179 are linked by their swirling arms. Known jointly as Arp 272, they are 450 million light-years from Earth, in the constellation of Hercules. They are a part of the Hercules Galaxy Cluster, which includes several pairs of interacting galaxies. The cluster is part of the Great Wall of galaxy clusters and superclusters—one of the largest known structures in the universe.

ANTENNAE ▶

The galaxies NGC 4038 and NGC 4039 began to collide about 700 million years ago. The cores of the two galaxies are shown in this image. Out of view are two long, faint streamers of stars that stretch away at either side and resemble an insect's antennae. The interaction of the galaxies has triggered a burst of star formation. Most of the star birth is in the compressed gas and dust cloud between the two cores.

COLLIDING GALAXIES

Galaxies have been evolving through a series of collisions, mergers, and interactions ever since the first ones formed billions of years ago. Over time, galaxies alter mass, size, and shape, changing from one type of galaxy to another. When two galaxies meet their stars rarely bump. Instead, the galaxies merge, their stars threading between each other. The gravity of one galaxy, however, can have a devastating effect on another—ripping away whole arms of stars, compressing gas clouds, and triggering star birth on a colossal scale.

▲ EARLY GALAXIES

The first stars were produced out of dense regions of matter when the universe was only about 500 million years old. By the time the universe was one billion years old, it was populated by dwarf galaxies. This young galaxy appears red because it is a vast distance away. It formed before the universe was three billion years old and is small enough to fit inside the central hub of the Milky Way.

▼ UGC 8335

This galaxy lies about 400 million light-years from Earth, in the constellation of Ursa Major. It consists of two interacting spiral galaxies. Their bright cores are linked by a bridge of stars, gas, and dust. Curving away from each core is a tail of gas and dust. This view of UGC 8335 is one of a collection of 59 images of merging galaxies taken by the Hubble Space Telescope and released on the telescope's 18th anniversary in April 2008.

ACTIVE GALAXIES

Some galaxies give off much more light than is expected from their stars alone. This is usually traced back to activity in their centers and for this reason they are called active galaxies. Most, if not all, galaxies have a black hole at their center. In an active galaxy, star material not only orbits the hole but falls in. This material forms a disklike ring around the hole and radiates intense energy. Material also jets out from either side of the hole. There are four main types of active galaxy: radio galaxy, quasar, blazar, and Seyfert galaxy.

❶ RADIO GALAXY
The radio galaxy Centaurus A lies 15 million light-years away, in the constellation of Centaurus. It is classified as a radio galaxy because of its powerful radio emission, particularly from two great lobes that jet out from above and below its central massive black hole. This view, which combines data from three telescopes, shows that the lobes emit X rays, too.

❷ QUASAR
One type of active galaxy is so bright and so distant that it appears as a starlike point of light. For this reason, these galaxies were called quasars, which was understood, these galaxies were called quasars, which is short for quasi-stellar object. Quasars are galaxies with incredibly brilliant cores. The core is so bright that it is very difficult to see the surrounding galaxy. Quasar HE0450-2958 is in the center, while above it is a cloud of gas, and below it is another galaxy.

❸ BLAZAR
The name blazar was coined in 1978 to describe some compact and powerful quasarlike objects that had been observed. Blazars are galaxies with their radio jets pointing towards Earth. In this image of blazar 3C 279, the white and red part is the center of the galaxy, and part of a radio jet is below.

❹ SEYFERT GALAXY
The Seyferts are relatively normal spiral galaxies, but with a compact center and radio lobes. Seyfert galaxy NGC 7742 has a yellow core and is called the Fried Egg Galaxy. Seyfert galaxies are named after Carl Seyfert who, in 1943, identified them as being different from other galaxies.

Seyferts and quasars have their dust rings tilted towards Earth

Radio galaxies have their dust rings side-on to Earth

Blazars have their dust rings face-on to Earth

❺ DIFFERENT VIEWS
The four types of active galaxy are thought to be the same type of object seen from different angles. The black hole is surrounded by a disk of star material and around this is a doughnut-shaped ring of dust and gas. Some disk material falling into the hole is fired out as two narrow jets. In Seyferts and quasars, the dust ring is angled to Earth; in radio galaxies, it is edge-on; in blazars, the view is front-on.

THE MILKY WAY

The Milky Way Galaxy is our galactic home. It is a disk-shaped system of gas and dust, and about 500 billion stars. It is classified as a barred spiral galaxy. Along with the rest of the solar system, we live about 27,000 light-years from the galaxy's center—a little more than halfway to the outer edge. From our position inside the galaxy, we see it as a milky path of light across Earth's nighttime sky, which is why we call it the Milky Way.

❶ PATH OF LIGHT
The Milky Way path of star-studded light that stretches across the night sky is our side-on view of the galaxy's disk. The brightest and broadest part of the path is the view into the galaxy's center. The remaining stars in the night sky are also part of the Milky Way Galaxy.

❷ FACE-ON VIEW
Our galaxy is disk-shaped with a bulging, roughly bar-shaped center that has spiral arms winding out of it. The bulge contains mainly older stars, while the arms are made of young and middle-aged ones. The galaxy is 100,000 light-years across and about 4,000 light-years thick. Each star follows its own path around the center, the galactic core, and the Sun takes 220 million years to complete one orbit.

❸ EDGE-ON VIEW
In this image, the galaxy is drawn edge-on and we are looking into the side of the disk. Completely surrounding the disk is a spherical halo consisting of individual old stars and more than 180 globular clusters, which are spherical collections of old stars. These stars and clusters follow long orbits that take them in toward and around the central bulge, then away again.

❹ CENTER OF THE MILKY WAY
Dense clouds of gas and dust obscure our view of the Milky Way's center. However, radio and X-ray observations reveal a star-packed heart with a supermassive black hole called Sagittarius A* at the very center. This X-ray image was taken by the Chandra space telescope. Sagittarius A*, which is at least three million times more massive than our Sun, is hidden from view in the lower right part of the central bright region.

Orion arm
Sun's orbit
Perseus arm

Galactic core
Obscured region

Sun
Norma arm

Sagittarius arm
Scutum-Crux arm

❺ MILKY WAY MAP

From inside the Milky Way, it is difficult to
make out the galaxy's structure. Our efforts to
find and then map its arms are also complicated
by the huge amounts of gas and dust in the galaxy's
disk. Radio and infrared observations suggest there are
two main arms (Perseus and Scutum-Crux), two minor
ones, and a part arm (Orion), which contains the Sun.

GALACTIC NEIGHBORS

The Milky Way and the Andromeda Galaxy are the two dominant members of a small cluster of more than 40 galaxies called the Local Group. The group occupies a volume of space shaped like a dumbbell that measures about 10 million light-years across. The galaxies in the Local Group are the Milky Way's nearest galactic neighbors. Even so, some members of the group, including Canis Major Dwarf—the closest to us at 25,000 light years—have been discovered only in recent years. This is because dust and gas in the Milky Way's disk blots out much of our view of what lies beyond.

❶ MILKY WAY
The Milky Way is a large barred spiral and the second most massive galaxy in the Local Group. Our solar system lies in the disk of the galaxy and is located within its Orion arm. Many of the group's smaller members orbit around the Milky Way—so far, 13 have been found. Some of these will eventually collide and merge with the Milky Way.

❷ ANDROMEDA
The largest member of the Local Group is the Andromeda Galaxy, which contains just over twice as many stars as the Milky Way. It is 2.5 million light-years away. When the distance to Andromeda was first measured about 90 years ago, the galaxy was the first body that was proved to be outside the Milky Way. About ten of the Local Group's smaller galaxies orbit around Andromeda.

❸ TRIANGULUM
The third largest member of the Local Group is the Triangulum Galaxy, which is about 3 million light-years away. It is a spiral galaxy whose arms are disjointed and split into parts. Many people can see the Andromeda Galaxy using the naked eye—for most of them, it is the farthest object they can see. In exceptionally good conditions, however, some people can see the Triangulum, which is more distant.

❹ LARGE MAGELLANIC CLOUD
The Large Magellanic Cloud (LMC) is the fourth largest member of the Local Group. It is about 20,000 light-years across, some 179,000 light-years away, and appears to orbit around the Milky Way every 1.5 billion years. Previously, the LMC might have been a barred spiral, but is now classified as an irregular galaxy. It is rich in star-forming regions and has a prominent central bar of stars.

❺ SMALL MAGELLANIC CLOUD
Like its larger namesake, the Small Magellanic Cloud (SMC) takes its name from the Portuguese explorer Ferdinand Magellan, who observed the two when circumnavigating the globe in the early 1500s. With a diameter of up to about 10,000 light years, the SMC is 7 billion times more massive than the Sun. Its distorted shape could be due to the Milky Way's gravity pulling on it.

❻ BARNARD'S GALAXY
This galaxy takes its name from the American astronomer E. E. Barnard, who discovered it in 1881 while using his telescope to search for comets. It is 1.7 million light-years away, is an irregular galaxy with a central bar, and contains only about 10 million stars. It has a similar composition and structure to the SMC and contains many young stars.

❼ SAGITTARIUS DWARF
This dwarf elliptical galaxy was discovered only in 1994. It is on the other side of the Milky Way's central nucleus to Earth, and, at a distance of 65,000 light-years, is our second closest companion galaxy. Its full name is Sagittarius Dwarf Elliptical Galaxy, but it is also known as SagDEG. The galaxy is relatively dust-free, with very old stars, and it is on a collision course with the Milky Way.

❽ SEXTANS A
At about 5.2 million light-years away, the Sextans A Galaxy is one of the most distant members of the Local Group. A new wave of star formation started in this dwarf irregular galaxy about 100 million years ago. Supernovae triggered even more star formation, and many bright, young, blue-white stars are visible in an expanding shell around the galaxy.

STAR BIRTH
This huge star-forming region of gas and dust is known as the Eagle Nebula. It is located in a spiral arm of the Milky Way Galaxy. At its center are the Pillars of Creation, three fingerlike regions several light-years long.

Stars

STAR QUALITY

There are trillions and trillions of stars in the universe. They are huge spinning globes of hot glowing gas made mainly of hydrogen and helium with small amounts of other elements. Much of a star's gas is squashed within its core, where it produces nuclear energy. From Earth, the stars can appear similar, but their characteristics, such as size, temperature, color, luminosity, and mass, differ from star to star. An individual star's characteristics also change as the star ages.

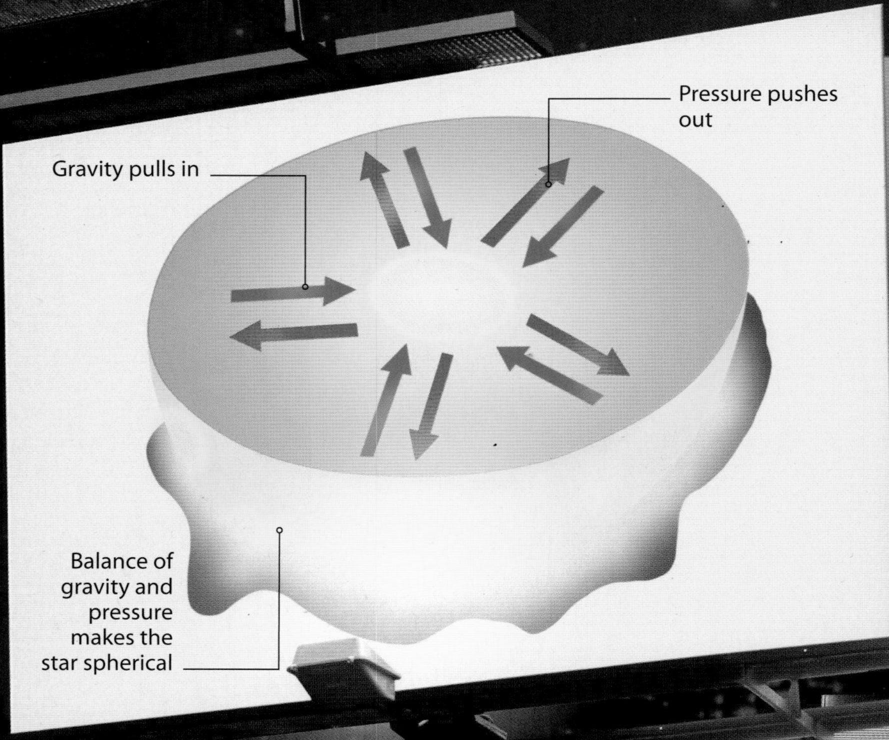

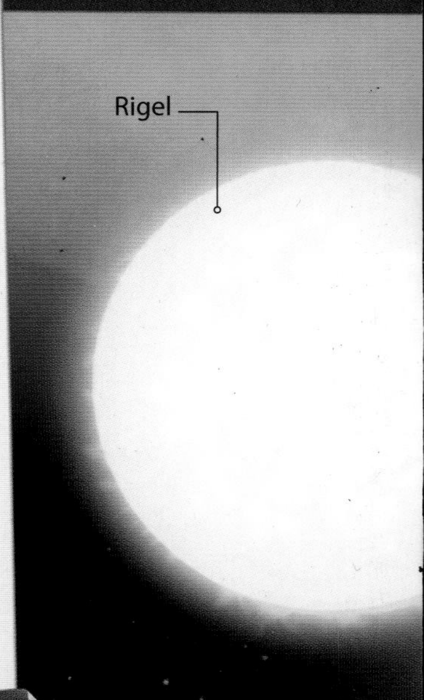

▲ COLOR AND TEMPERATURE

A star's color indicates its temperature, and as the star's temperature changes, so does the color. Stars are classified according to their color and temperature. There are seven main types: blue stars (72,000°F, 40,000°C), blue-white stars (54,000°F, 30,000°C), white stars (19,800°F, 11,000°C), yellow-white stars (13,500°F, 7,500°C), yellow stars (10,800°F, 6,000°C), orange stars (9,000°F, 5,000°C), and red stars (7,200°F, 4,000°C).

Gravity pulls in

Pressure pushes out

Rigel

Balance of gravity and pressure makes the star spherical

▲ GRAVITY AND PRESSURE

A star's gravity pulls the star's gas in toward its center. At the same time, the pressure of the dense core pushes out the material. The two forces balance each other out and maintain the star's size. Most stars are nearly spherical, though rapid spin makes them bulge around the equator. When two stars are very close, the gravity of each one pulls on the other, making their shapes distorted.

The amount of light a star produces is called its luminosity. The most luminous stars emit more than 6 million times the Sun's light, and the least emit less than one ten-thousandth. Luminosity is an indication of the actual brightness of the star and is different from the brightness seen from Earth. If the Sun were farther away, it would appear dimmer even though it would have the same luminosity.

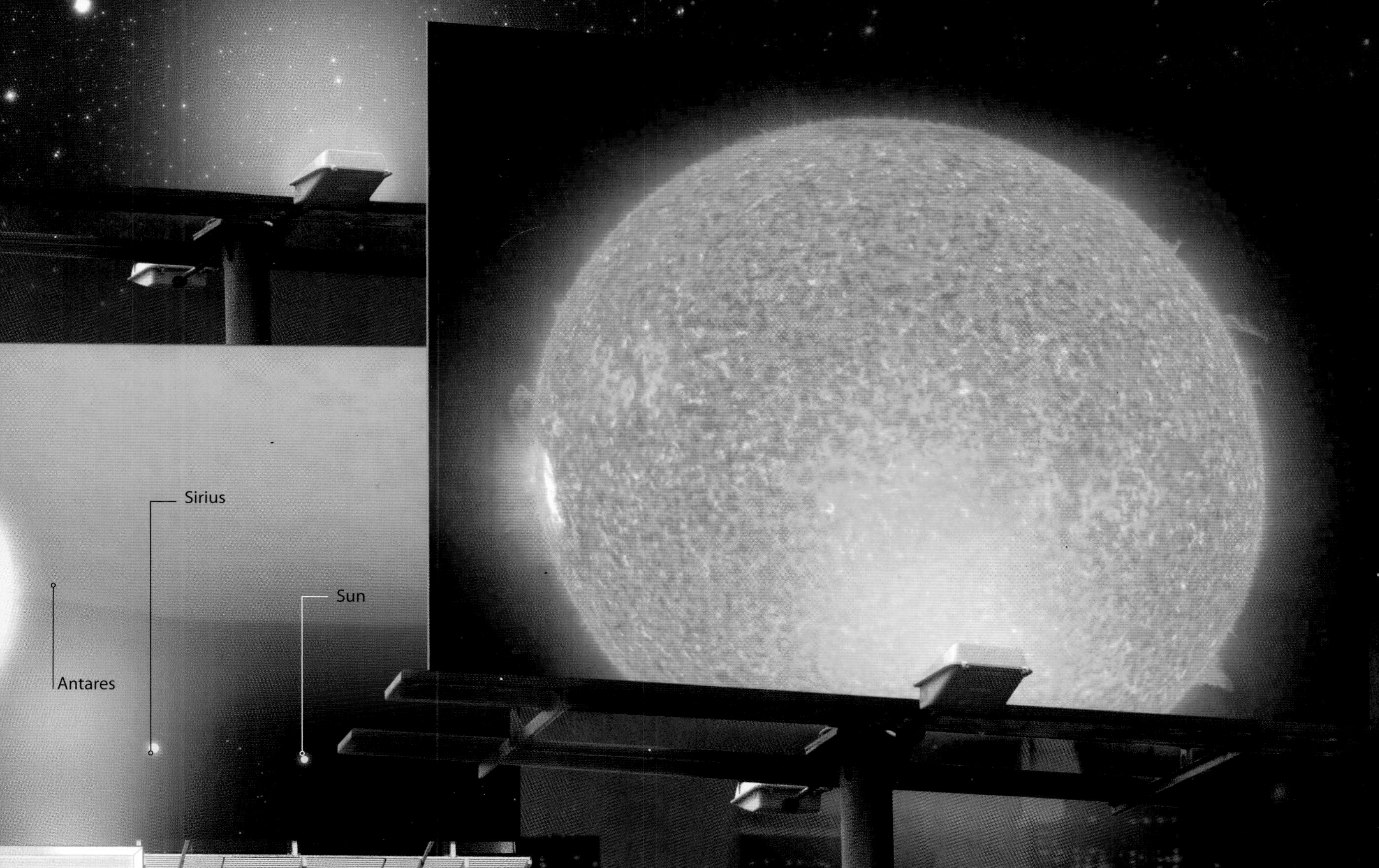

Sirius

Sun

Antares

▲ **STAR MASS**
The amount of material a star is made of is its mass. It determines the length and the course of a star's life. The Sun is said to be made of one solar mass and other stars are measured in multiples or fractions of this. The most massive stars are about 100 times the Sun's mass, while the least are just one-tenth of the Sun's mass.

▲ **STAR SIZE**
A star's size can vary considerably during the course of its life. Large stars, such as Antares, are several hundred times bigger than the Sun. The largest of all are more than 1,000 times our star's width, whereas the smallest are about one-hundredth of it. A star's size is related to the density of its material. Two stars can have the same mass, but take up different volumes of space.

THE SUN

The Sun is our closest star, and it heats and lights our planet. This blisteringly hot, incandescent globe has a surface temperature of 9,900°F (5,500°C) and this gives it its yellow color. Measuring 864,900 miles (1.4 million km) across, the Sun is not a solid object. It is made of gas all the way through, with its temperature, density, and pressure increasing toward its center. Made of almost three-quarters hydrogen, about a quarter helium, and small amounts of 90 or so other elements, it is all held together by gravity.

❶ GRANULATION

The Sun's visible surface is the photosphere. It is mottled by granulation and has the appearance of orange peel. This effect is achieved by spheres of hot gas, about 620 miles (1,000 km) across, rushing up to the surface at about 0.3 miles (0.5 km) per second. Here, they radiate away their energy and then sink back, once they have cooled. Each granulation typically lasts for eight minutes.

❷ SUNSPOTS

Dark spots appear periodically on the Sun's photosphere. They are relatively cool regions produced as the Sun's magnetic field interrupts rising heat. A single spot can be wider than Earth. The central, darkest, and coolest part is the umbra, and surrounding this is the penumbra. A typical large spot lasts for about two months. The Sun's spottiness varies over an 11-year cycle.

❸ SPICULES

Short-lived jets of gas continually leap up from the photosphere. They are tiny compared to the Sun, but each is about 310 miles (500 km) wide and up to 6,200 miles (10,000 km) long. They shoot upward at around 12.4 miles (20 km) per second. At any one time, the Sun has about 70,000 spicules, each lasting for up to 10 minutes. Together, they resemble blades of grass blowing in the wind.

❹ FLARES AND PROMINENCES

Massive bursts of energy, called flares, explode out of the surface at speeds of up to 620 miles (1,000 km) per second. The flare material is heated to temperatures of around 18 million °F (10 million °C). Huge visible regions of relatively cool gas that loop and arch from the surface are known as prominences. They extend out into the solar corona and can last for several months.

❺ CORONA

Beyond the Sun's photosphere is its atmosphere, which is normally invisible and can only be seen during a total solar eclipse. However, it can now be monitored using spacecraft. The part next to the Sun's surface is the chromosphere. Beyond is the corona, a low-density region one million times fainter than the photosphere, which extends out for millions of miles. Material continuously streaming from it is called the solar wind.

❻ INSIDE THE SUN

At the very center of the Sun is its core. This extends out about a quarter of the Sun's radius, has a density 150 times that of water, and a temperature of around 27 million °F (15 million °C). In this gaseous region, nuclear reactions convert hydrogen to helium. This produces energy, which moves to the surface where it is released.

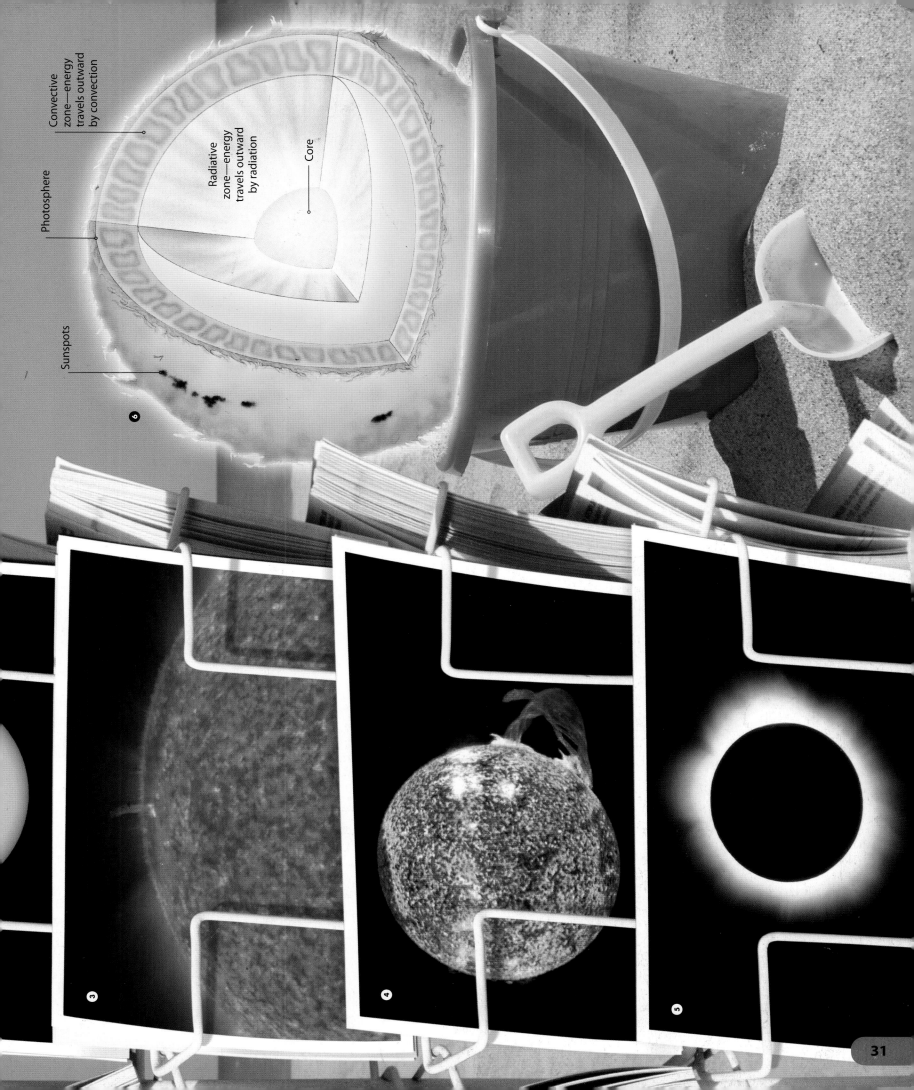

Convective zone—energy travels outward by convection

Photosphere

Radiative zone—energy travels outward by radiation

Core

Sunspots

6

3

4

5

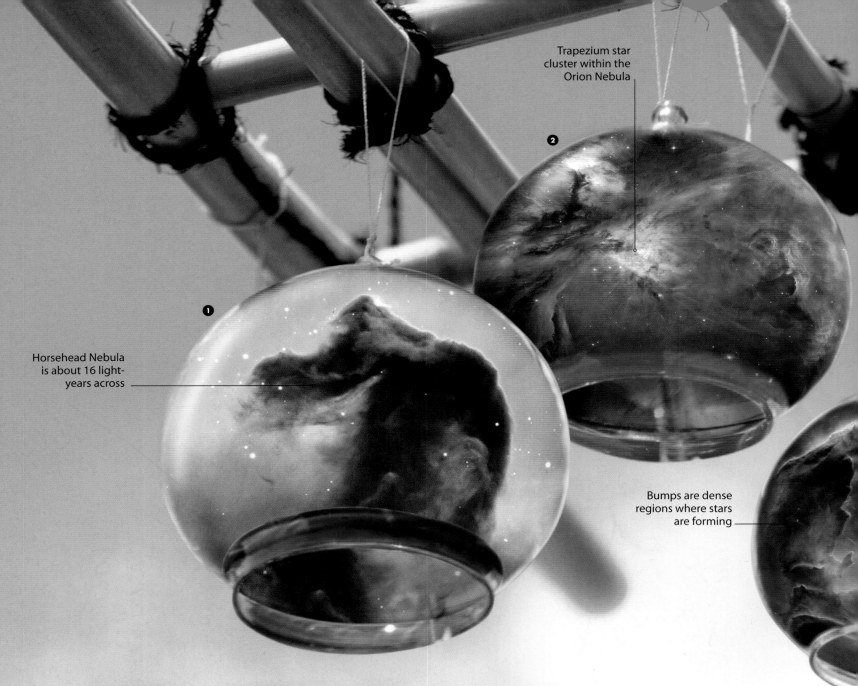

Trapezium star cluster within the Orion Nebula

❶

❷

Horsehead Nebula is about 16 light-years across

Bumps are dense regions where stars are forming

GAS AND DUST

Galaxies are much more than stars. They contain vast amounts of gas and dust that exist between the stars. This interstellar material is not evenly distributed and some of it is sparsely spread out, but much is in the form of huge, dense clouds. These clouds consist of mainly hydrogen gas, with helium and dust. Temperature defines the appearance of the clouds and the processes going on inside. A trigger, such as a collision with another cloud or a shockwave from a supernova explosion, can start star formation in some of the cooler clouds.

❶ HORSEHEAD NEBULA

This dark, dense cloud is shaped like a horse's head. Classified as a dark nebula, it is a cool cloud of dust and hydrogen. Its mass is about 300 times that of the Sun. The horse's head is visible because it is silhouetted against a brighter background. It rears out of a larger dark cloud that includes young stars in the process of formation. The nebula is in the constellation of Orion, located below the hunter's belt.

❷ ORION NEBULA

One of the best known and closest star-forming regions is the Orion Nebula. It is also the brightest in Earth's night sky. At its heart, is the Trapezium star cluster, which is about 30,000 years old. It is principally the ultraviolet radiation from its four most brilliant stars that causes the whole nebula to glow. The nebula is about 30 light-years across, but is part of a much larger cloud system.

❸ PILLARS OF CREATION

These three columns of gas and dust are several light years long. Known as the Pillars of Creation, they are a very small part of a huge star-forming region, the Eagle Nebula, which is located within one of the spiral arms of the Milky Way Galaxy. The nebula is a vast cloud of gas and dust that also includes young stars that have already formed and regions where new stars are being born.

Keyhole Nebula
within the vast
Carina Nebula

❻ STAR BIRTH REGION

This huge star birth nebula is in the Large
Magellanic Cloud, one of the Milky Way's
galactic neighbors. It is located near the
star cluster NGC 2074. Ultraviolet radiation
from the hot, young stars in the cluster is
slowly eroding away the nebula and has
sculpted the pillars and filaments of gas
and dust. The seahorse-shaped pillar at
lower right is about 20 light-years long.

Nebula near
star cluster
NGC 2074

IRS4 is about 2,000
light-years away in
the constellation
of Cygnus

❹ ETA CARINA NEBULA

The Eta Carina Nebula is one of the largest
and brightest interstellar clouds known.
It is more than 300 light-years across and
contains some of the most massive stars
discovered. Many of these are within a region
known as the Keyhole Nebula. They include
the star Eta Carinae, which is 100 times more
massive than the Sun. This image, which
shows only part of the nebula, was taken
by the Hubble Space Telescope.

❺ NEWBORN STAR

Material streams out of the newborn star IRS4, which
was born only about 100,000 years ago. The gas and
dust nearest the star shines brightly because the star's
heat changes the hydrogen atoms and light is emitted.
Brown dwarf stars are within the outer material. They
don't have enough mass for nuclear reactions in their
cores and will never shine as brightly as other stars.

◄ PLEIADES

The best known and one of the nearest open clusters is the Pleiades, in the constellation of Taurus. This group of stars is 440 light-years away and it is estimated that there are about 5,000 stars in the cluster. The core of the Pleiades is about eight light-years across and dominated by very bright, blue-white stars. The cluster is slowly losing members and is expected to disperse completely in the next 250 million years.

LIVING TOGETHER

When stars are produced, they are not formed singly but in clusters. There are two types of cluster. Loose-knit, "open" clusters are relatively young and some are forming in our galaxy's disk now. The stars in these clusters will eventually drift apart. Much denser, "globular" clusters were formed when the galaxy was born and are still together. These are within the galactic halo and orbit the galaxy's nucleus. The Milky Way Galaxy contains about 180 globular clusters and many thousands of open clusters.

◄ BUTTERFLY CLUSTER

The outline of this open cluster of stars is said to look like a butterfly with open wings. The cluster is about 12 light-years across and 1,600 light-years away. Each of its stars is in orbit around the cluster's center of mass, and, like the rest of the Milky Way's open clusters, the whole cluster is orbiting the nucleus of the galaxy. Most of its stars are blue, but the brightest star in the cluster is an orange supergiant.

GLOBULAR CLUSTER ▶

M13, sometimes called the Great Globular Cluster, is 25,000 light-years away, in the constellation of Hercules. Globulars are spherical, with more stars and are bigger than open clusters. This close-packed collection of about four million stars occupies a volume of space 170 light-years across. The cluster was formed more than 13 billion years ago. It follows a very elongated orbit around the nucleus of the Milky Way, and takes about 100 million years to complete one circuit.

◀ COMPANIONS

The Sun, like about half of all nearby stars, is alone. The other nearby stars exist alongside one or more stars. Almost a third are binaries—two stars bound together by each other's gravity. About 15 percent are triplets, and the rest are quads and quins. The bright star Albireo appears to be single, but consists of a bright, golden giant star and a fainter, blue-dwarf star close together in the sky. Some astronomers believe that they are gravitationally bound together.

CLOSE PAIR ▼

Some binary stars, such as the white dwarf (right) orbiting a brown dwarf star in this artwork, are so close that their separation is only about the diameter of the largest star. Under these circumstances, material from the outer part of one star can be pulled away by the strong magnetic field of the other. This mass transfer changes the physical states of the two stars and effects how they evolve. The gravity of each star can also pull on the other star, changing its shape from spherical to elliptical.

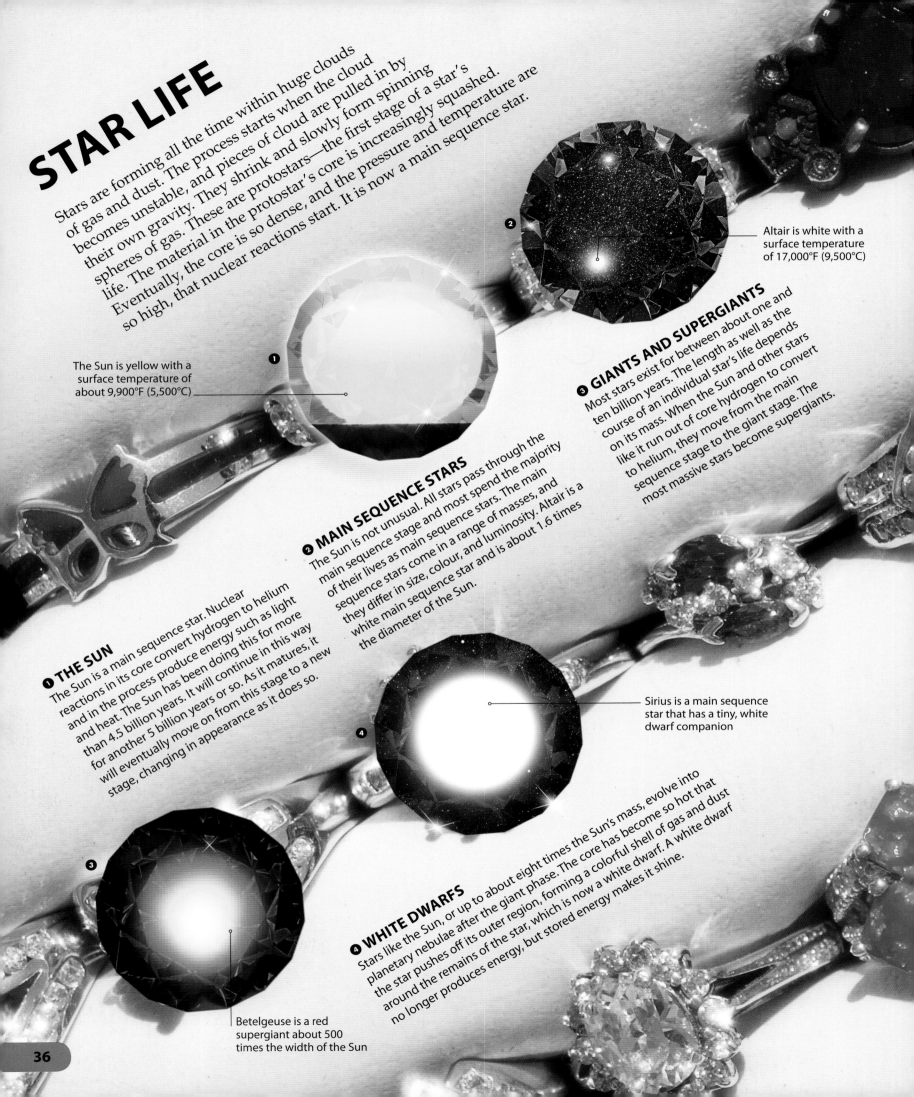

STAR LIFE

Stars are forming all the time within huge clouds of gas and dust. The process starts when the cloud becomes unstable, and pieces of cloud are pulled in by their own gravity. They shrink and slowly form spinning spheres of gas. These are protostars—the first stage of a star's life. The material in the protostar's core is increasingly squashed. Eventually, the core is so dense, and the pressure and temperature are so high, that nuclear reactions start. It is now a main sequence star.

The Sun is yellow with a surface temperature of about 9,900°F (5,500°C)

Altair is white with a surface temperature of 17,000°F (9,500°C)

❸ GIANTS AND SUPERGIANTS

Most stars exist for between about one and ten billion years. The length as well as the course of an individual star's life depends on its mass. When the Sun and other stars like it run out of core hydrogen to convert to helium, they move from the main sequence stage to the giant stage. The most massive stars become supergiants.

❷ MAIN SEQUENCE STARS

The Sun is not unusual. All stars pass through the main sequence stage and most spend the majority of their lives as main sequence stars. The main sequence stars come in a range of masses, and they differ in size, colour, and luminosity. Altair is a white main sequence star and is about 1.6 times the diameter of the Sun.

❶ THE SUN

The Sun is a main sequence star. Nuclear reactions in its core convert hydrogen to helium and in the process produce energy such as light and heat. The Sun has been doing this for more than 4.5 billion years. It will continue in this way for another 5 billion years or so. As it matures, it will eventually move on from this stage to a new stage, changing in appearance as it does so.

Sirius is a main sequence star that has a tiny, white dwarf companion

❹ WHITE DWARFS

Stars like the Sun, or up to about eight times the Sun's mass, evolve into planetary nebulae after the giant phase. The core has become so hot that the star pushes off its outer region, forming a colorful shell of gas and dust around the remains of the star, which is now a white dwarf. A white dwarf no longer produces energy, but stored energy makes it shine.

Betelgeuse is a red supergiant about 500 times the width of the Sun

❺ ANT NEBULA

The Ant Nebula, so named because it looks like the head and central body of a common garden ant, is a planetary nebula. Material is moving away from the central star at around 2.25 million mph (3.6 million kph). Most is in the lobes which stretch out to a distance of more than 1.5 light-years. The uneven way that the material has been expelled suggests there could be two stars in the center.

Lobes of expelled
star material

❼ RED RECTANGLE

The unusual shape of the Red Rectangle Nebula is due to a pair of central stars. A dense disk of material around the two stars has restricted the flow of the expelled gas. The nebula isn't a rectangle at all and only appears so because we see it from the side. It consists of rings of material moving outward on opposite sides of the stars.

Two central stars
orbit their common
center of mass

❻ CAT'S EYE NEBULA

The intricate nature of the Cat's Eye Nebula is revealed in this image. It has been produced by combining data from two space telescopes, the Chandra X-ray Observatory and the Hubble Space Telescope. The purple-colored regions, only seen in X-ray light, are hot gas. The red and green regions, seen at optical wavelengths, are cooler gas.

Eleven different rings of
material have been ejected
by the central star

❽ HELIX NEBULA

One of the brightest and closest planetary nebulae is the Helix Nebula. This image shows it in infrared and optical light. Infrared images have revealed thousands of tadpole-shaped gaseous knots, several thousand million miles long. The dying star in its center is destined to be a white dwarf. It will then slowly fade and cool, until it is a cold, dark cinder in space—a black dwarf.

Helix Nebula main
ring is 1.5 light-years
in diameter

EXPLOSIVE END

The nature and timing of a star's death is determined by its mass. Stars more massive than the Sun have shorter lives and can die after just a few million rather than a few billion years. Some massive stars end their lives abruptly. Those made of more than about eight times the Sun's mass end their lives in explosive fashion. Their outer material is blasted into space leaving a small core behind. Eventually, the expelled material will help create new stars.

❶ SUPERNOVA

When a massive star has run out of gas to convert, its core collapses and much of the star is blown off in a colossal explosion. This releases huge amounts of energy making the star extremely bright. This is known as a supernova. The original star's core is left behind after the explosion and its fate depends on its mass. On average, a supernova is likely to go off every few hundred years in a typical galaxy.

❷ NEUTRON STAR

If the core left behind by a supernova is between about 1.4 and three times the mass of the Sun, gravity forces the core to collapse. It forms a neutron star—a city-sized sphere which emits beams of energy that sweep across space as the star spins rapidly. These are the smallest, densest stars we can detect. A neutron star discovered by its beams is known as a pulsar.

❸ SUPERNOVA REMNANT

The material pushed off during a supernova explosion is known as a supernova remnant. It moves out from the site of the explosion and away from the leftover core and spreads out slowly into space. The material in the Vela supernova remnant, shown here, is from a star that exploded about 11,000 years ago. The star's core became a pulsar which spins around 11 times a second.

❹ BLACK HOLE

A supernova core made of more than about three times the mass of the Sun doesn't stop collapsing at the neutron star stage. It continues to collapse, becoming denser and smaller until it is a hole in space—a black hole. Its gravitation is so strong that even light or other forms of radiation cannot escape from it. The black hole cannot be detected directly, but is identified by the effect it has on objects around it.

❺ ETA CARINAE

One of the most massive stars discovered in the night sky is Eta Carinae—it is 100 times more massive than the Sun. It lies at the center of a dumbbell-shaped cloud of gas and dust. The huge lobes of material were observed being ejected in 1841. The star erupts irregularly, and when it does, its brightness increases significantly. It is expected that Eta Carinae will end its life in one final giant eruption as a supernova.

❻ STELLAR RECYCLING

Supernova remnant material can be used to create new stars. It slowly mixes with material shed by other stars, as well as with hydrogen gas that exists between the stars. Over millions more years, this mixed material collects together by gravity into vast, cold, dark clouds. These clouds produce new stars, which, in turn, will scatter material that could go on to produce a further generation of stars.

Nuclear reactions in star produces heavier elements

Fragments of cloud condense to form stars

Mature star sheds material

Clouds form from star and interstellar material

EXOPLANETS

At least one in every 20 stars in the sky has planets orbiting it. Before 1992, the Sun was the only star with planets that we knew. Hundreds of planets orbiting other stars are now known. They are called extrasolar planets, or exoplanets. The first to be discovered were a pair of planets around the pulsar B1257+12. The first found orbiting a star like the Sun was in 1995, around 51 Pegasi.

❷ FOMALHAUT B

A huge ring of gas and dust measuring 21.5 billion miles (34.6 billion km) across surrounds Fomalhaut. The star's light has been blocked so the ring can be seen in this image. Within the ring is the exoplanet Fomalhaut b, which is about 10 times farther from its star than Saturn is from the Sun. It takes 872 years to orbit Fomalhaut and is three times the mass of Jupiter.

❶ DISCOVERY

Exoplanets are difficult to detect because they are relatively small objects and located next to much larger and much brighter stars. Most have been found by studying the spectra of stars over time to detect wobbles in their motion caused by the gravity of orbiting planets. This view combines separate images of the brown dwarf star 2M1207 and its planet 2M1207b.

❸ HR 8799B

Exoplanet HR 8799b was discovered in images taken by Earth-based telescopes in 2007. It is the outermost of three planets orbiting the star HR 8799 and estimated to be at least seven times the mass of Jupiter and about the same diameter. It was imaged by the Hubble Space Telescope in 1998, but went undetected. Its 1998 and 2008 positions are shown in the bottom right corner of this Hubble view.

❶ Brown dwarf star 2M1207

Planet 2M1207b

❷

❸ 1998 — 2008 position

❹ The red glow in the center is a young star

The disk is about 99 percent gas and 1 percent dust

SEQUENCE COUNT

0 2 1

The huge disks of gas and dust that astronomers have discovered surrounding some stars will go on to form planets. Called protoplanetary disks, they are like the disk of material that surrounded the newly formed Sun and that produced Earth and the other solar system planets. The four shown here are within the Orion Nebula.

❺ MASSIVE WORLDS

More than 40 stars are known to have more than one planet orbiting them. The red dwarf star Gliese 581 has four, while the star 55 Cancri has five, the most known so far. Most exoplanets discovered so far are typically about the same mass as Jupiter. Some are more Earthlike in the amount of material they are made of. Gliese 581e is one of the least massive—it is at least 1.9 times the mass of Earth.

An artist's impression of an exoplanet orbiting Gliese 581

The central star is young, roughly one million years old

The disk is about eight times the diameter of the solar system

CONSTELLATIONS

All the stars except the Sun are so far away that they appear like pinpoints of light and seem to be the same distance from us. Astronomers identify individual stars and find their way about the night sky by using a system of constellations. There are 88 constellations, and each is a straight-edged area of sky that includes a made-up pattern in the shape of a person, creature, or object. The patterns are formed by linking the brightest stars with imaginary lines.

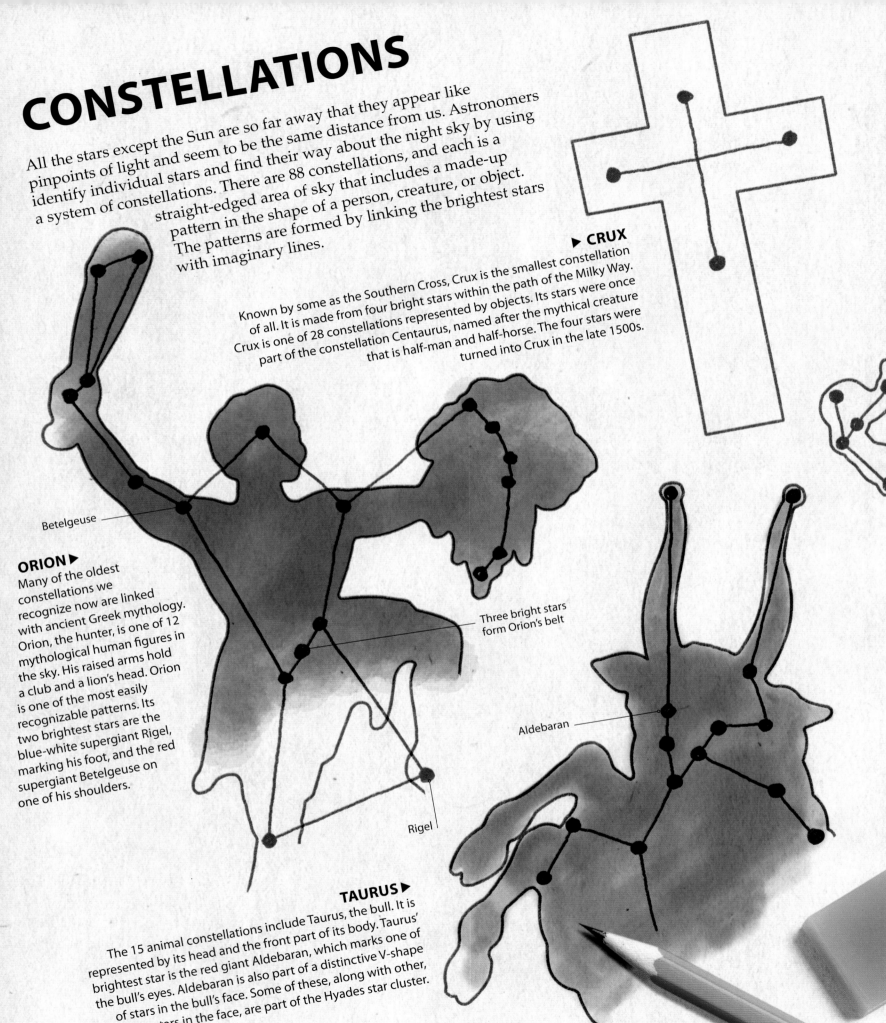

▶ CRUX

Known by some as the Southern Cross, Crux is the smallest constellation of all. It is made from four bright stars within the path of the Milky Way. Crux is one of 28 constellations represented by objects. Its stars were once part of the constellation Centaurus, named after the mythical creature that is half-man and half-horse. The four stars were turned into Crux in the late 1500s.

Betelgeuse

ORION ▶

Many of the oldest constellations we recognize now are linked with ancient Greek mythology. Orion, the hunter, is one of 12 mythological human figures in the sky. His raised arms hold a club and a lion's head. Orion is one of the most easily recognizable patterns. Its two brightest stars are the blue-white supergiant Rigel, marking his foot, and the red supergiant Betelgeuse on one of his shoulders.

Three bright stars form Orion's belt

Aldebaran

Rigel

TAURUS ▶

The 15 animal constellations include Taurus, the bull. It is represented by its head and the front part of its body. Taurus' brightest star is the red giant Aldebaran, which marks one of the bull's eyes. Aldebaran is also part of a distinctive V-shape of stars in the bull's face. Some of these, along with other, fainter stars in the face, are part of the Hyades star cluster.

Red supergiant Antares marks the heart of Scorpius

◀ SCORPIUS

The backdrop to the path of the Sun, Moon, and planets across the stars is made up of 12 constellations, including Scorpius and Taurus. Together they are known as the zodiac, a term that derives from the Greek word for animal. Apart from Libra, which is a set of scales, the zodiac constellations all represent living or mythological creatures. Scorpius was the mythological scorpion that killed Orion with its sting.

URSA MAJOR ▶

Most constellations have two names—their Latin name and their common name. Ursa Major is commonly known as the great bear. It is one of two bears in the sky: the second is Ursa Minor, the little bear. They are found in the sky above Earth's northern hemisphere and, unlike real bears, both have long tails. The two are seen all year through by observers in the northern hemisphere.

Ursa Major is the third-largest constellation

Dubhe, the star farthest from Earth in the Big Dipper, is 125 light-years away

▶ OPTICAL ILLUSION

The stars in a particular pattern only appear to be associated. In fact, they are unrelated and at vastly differing distances from Earth. Here, the seven stars known as the Big Dipper, and which form the tail and rear of Ursa Major, appear on the black screen as they appear from Earth. When viewed from another direction, they are seen to vary in distance from Earth and create a different pattern.

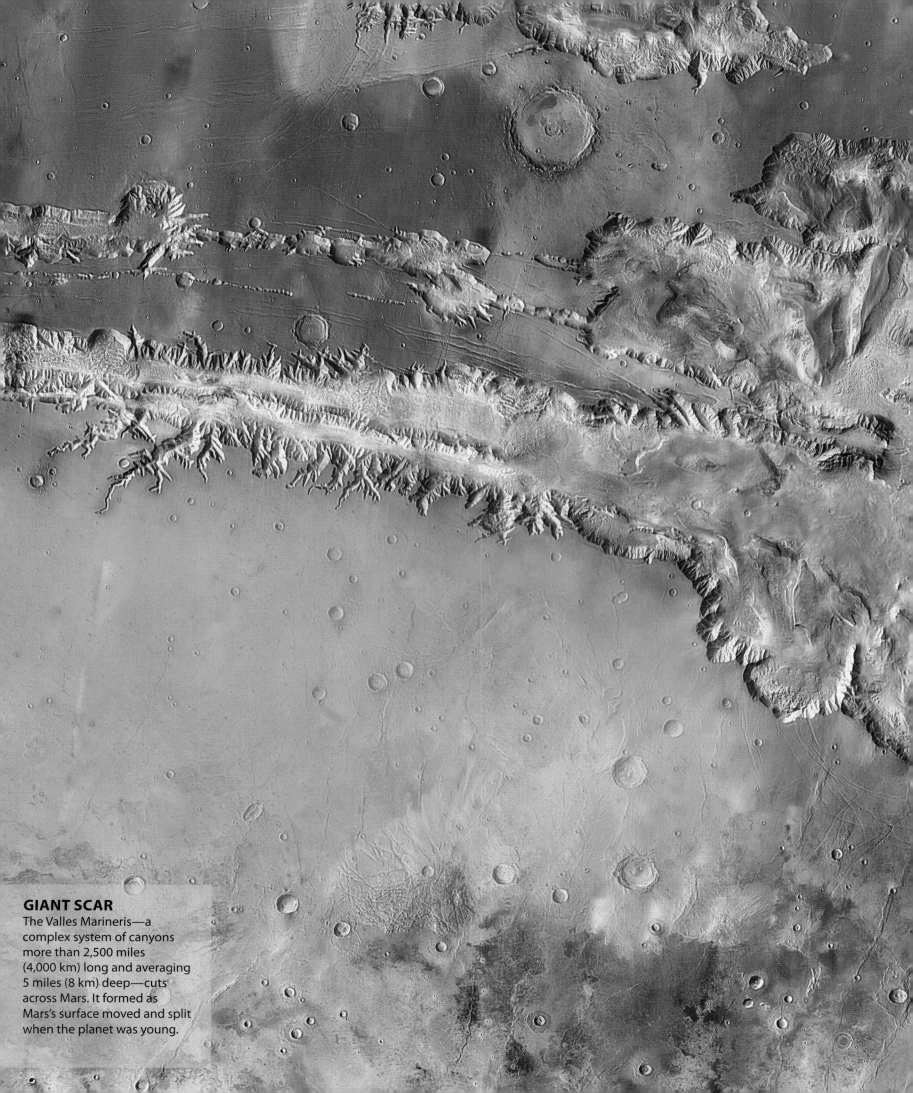

GIANT SCAR
The Valles Marineris—a complex system of canyons more than 2,500 miles (4,000 km) long and averaging 5 miles (8 km) deep—cuts across Mars. It formed as Mars's surface moved and split when the planet was young.

The solar system

THE SUN'S FAMILY

The Sun and the large family of objects that orbit around it are known as the solar system. The Sun is the biggest of these bodies—next in size are eight planets. Closest to the Sun are the rock and metal worlds of Mercury, Venus, Earth, and Mars. More distant are four giant-sized planets with deep atmospheres of gas—Jupiter, Saturn, Uranus, and Neptune. These are outnumbered by trillions of small bodies: dwarf planets, moons, asteroids, comets, and Kuiper Belt objects.

❶ THE SUN

The center of the solar system is occupied by the Sun. This enormous object is a star—a huge glowing ball of mainly hydrogen gas powered by nuclear reactions in its core. The Sun is made up of 99 percent of all the system's material. The star's huge size creates a powerful gravitational force that holds all the other family members in orbit around it. The Sun and its family formed about 4.6 billion years ago from a vast spinning cloud of gas and dust. Material pulled into the center formed the Sun. Some material settled into a disk around the Sun in which the planets formed over millions of years.

❷ MERCURY

At 3,029 miles (4,875 km) across, Mercury is less than half Earth's size and the smallest planet. It is also the closest to the Sun and takes the least time to orbit the Sun—it takes just 88 days to complete one circuit. Mercury's surface is gray, dry, and covered with impact craters. The planet is named after the swift-footed messenger to the Roman gods.

❸ VENUS

Even though Venus is not the closest planet to the Sun, it is the hottest. A dense atmosphere of carbon dioxide around Venus traps the Sun's heat, which warms up the planet's surface. Although Venus basks in the Sun's rays, the thick sulphur-dioxide cloud cover means the Sun is invisible from the surface. Venus is also the slowest-spinning planet, turning around once on its axis every 243 days—longer than the time it takes to orbit the Sun.

❹ EARTH

Earth is the third farthest planet from the Sun. It has one moon, takes a year to complete an orbit around the Sun, and takes 23.9 hours to make one spin on its axis. Earth is the only planet known to have liquid water. The oceans that cover much of its surface are visible from space. Our planet is also the only place in the universe known to have life.

❺ MARS

Beyond Earth is Mars. It is about one and a half times farther from the Sun than Earth and about half our planet's size. It orbits the Sun in 687 days and spins round once every 24.6 hours. Mars has a very thin carbon-dioxide atmosphere, and its cold, dry surface is clearly visible from space. Two small moons orbit around the planet.

Sun

Jupiter

Earth

Mercury

Venus

Asteroid Belt

Uranus

❻ ASTEROID BELT

Millions of asteroids orbit the Sun between Mars and Jupiter. Together, these small rocky bodies occupy a doughnut-shaped region of space known as the Asteroid Belt or Main Belt. Each asteroid follows its own path around the Sun and takes four to five years to complete one orbit. Most are irregular in shape and less than 18.6 miles (30 km) across. Asteroids are unused material from when the planets formed.

❼ JUPITER

The second biggest object in the solar system, Jupiter is also the largest planet—11 Earths would fit across its face. The fifth planet from the Sun, Jupiter is the innermost of the giant planets. It is the fastest-spinning planet, taking just under ten hours to make one spin. It takes 11.9 years to complete one orbit around the Sun.

❽ SATURN

A complex system of rings around Saturn makes it one of the most easily recognizable planets. It is the second largest planet and sixth in distance from the Sun. The time taken for a planet to orbit the Sun increases with distance—Saturn takes 29.5 years. Its orbit, like those of the other seven planets, is elliptical (a stretched circle). Like the other planets, it travels anticlockwise around the Sun.

❾ URANUS

The planet Uranus appears to roll along its orbit around the Sun. The planet is tilted over by 98° and, although its rings and moons circle its equator, when we look at the planet they seem to go around from top to bottom. Uranus is twice as far away from the Sun as Saturn and takes 84 years to complete one orbit.

❿ NEPTUNE

The most distant planet of all and the one that takes longest to orbit the Sun is Neptune. On average, this deep-blue world is 2.8 billion miles (4.5 billion km) from the Sun and it takes 164.9 years to complete one circuit. As Neptune travels along its orbit, it completes one rotation on its axis in just over 16 hours. Named after the Roman god of the seas, Neptune is also the coldest planet.

⓫ KUIPER BELT

A region of mainly icy objects known as the Kuiper Belt extends out from beyond Neptune's orbit. The largest members of the belt are dwarf planets, and include Eris and Pluto. The other members are known as Kuiper Belt objects. Beyond the belt is the Oort Cloud, a vast sphere made up of more than a trillion comets.

Kuiper Belt objects

Mars

Saturn

Neptune

ROCKY PLANETS

Mercury, Venus, Earth, and Mars are the smallest planets and the four closest to the Sun. Together, they are known as the terrestrial or rocky planets. Yet, the description "rocky" is misleading because the planets are a mix of mainly rock and metal. The four formed at the same time and from the same material, but they are very different worlds today. Earth has liquid water and life, Venus's volcanic surface is hidden by clouds, red Mars has ice-cold deserts, and Mercury has an ancient, cratered surface.

❶ PLANETARY INTERIORS
Inside the planets, their material is loosely divided into layers. When the planets were young, iron and nickel sank towards the center and their lighter rocks floated on top. Over time, the planets cooled and their metal cores either completely or partially solidified. Venus and Earth have similar interiors, and compared to the other three, Mercury is very rich in metals.

❷ MERCURY
The surface of gray, lifeless Mercury has hardly changed over the past three billion years. The planet is covered with impact craters formed by asteroids that smashed into it when it was young. Mercury is closest to the Sun, but the planet's thin and temporary atmosphere can't hang onto its daytime heat. Mercury has the greatest temperature range of all the planets: a scorching 806°F (430°C) in the day, but a super-cold -292°F (-180°C) at night.

❸ VENUS'S ATMOSPHERE
A thick and unbroken layer of clouds surrounds Venus. The clouds are made of sulphuric acid droplets and hang within a carbon-dioxide rich atmosphere. The atmosphere traps in heat, like glass in a greenhouse. The surface temperature is constantly about 867°F (464°C); it hardly varies from day to night, and no matter where you are on the planet.

❹ VENUS'S SURFACE
A little smaller than Earth, Venus is a gloomy place. Its surface is permanently overcast because most of the sunlight reaching the planet is reflected by its clouds. The planet is mainly low-lying plains made of volcanic lava that erupted onto the land hundreds of millions of years ago.

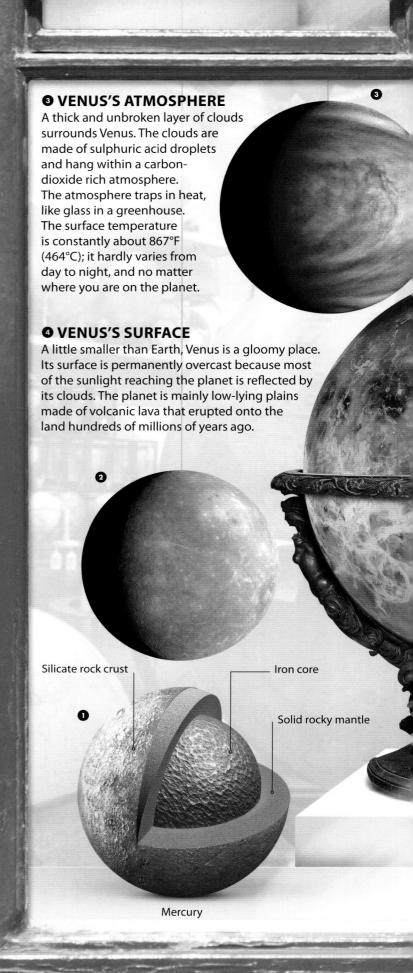

Silicate rock crust

Iron core

Solid rocky mantle

Mercury

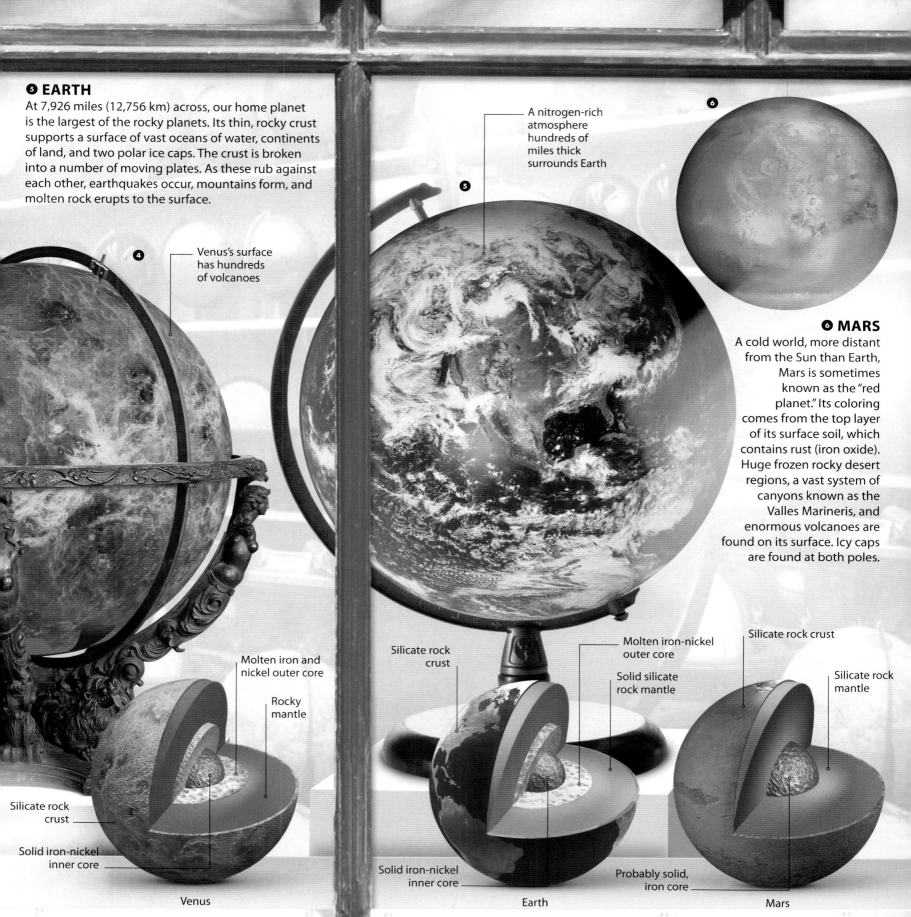

❺ EARTH

At 7,926 miles (12,756 km) across, our home planet is the largest of the rocky planets. Its thin, rocky crust supports a surface of vast oceans of water, continents of land, and two polar ice caps. The crust is broken into a number of moving plates. As these rub against each other, earthquakes occur, mountains form, and molten rock erupts to the surface.

A nitrogen-rich atmosphere hundreds of miles thick surrounds Earth

❹ Venus's surface has hundreds of volcanoes

❻ MARS

A cold world, more distant from the Sun than Earth, Mars is sometimes known as the "red planet." Its coloring comes from the top layer of its surface soil, which contains rust (iron oxide). Huge frozen rocky desert regions, a vast system of canyons known as the Valles Marineris, and enormous volcanoes are found on its surface. Icy caps are found at both poles.

Molten iron and nickel outer core

Rocky mantle

Silicate rock crust

Solid iron-nickel inner core

Venus

Silicate rock crust

Molten iron-nickel outer core

Solid silicate rock mantle

Solid iron-nickel inner core

Earth

Silicate rock crust

Silicate rock mantle

Probably solid, iron core

Mars

IMPACT!

When the planets were young, they were bombarded by asteroids—pieces of rocky material left over from the planet-making process. The asteroids formed craters: circular hollows that took shape as the impact of the asteroid blasted out surface material. Many millions of these craters are still intact. Earth suffered many impacts, but only a few craters remain because the planet's surface has changed so much. One big impact with Earth is believed to have formed the Moon.

BOMBARDED WORLDS ▶

An asteroid hits a planet at about 20 miles (30 km) per second. Smashing into the surface rock, it forms a crater about 10–15 times wider than the asteroid. The impact breaks up the asteroid and pulverizes the surrounding surface rock, which is ejected in all directions. The most intense period of bombardment was about 3.5 billion years ago. Although the rate of impact has decreased, it hasn't stopped. A 0.6-miles (1-km) wide or bigger asteroid hits Earth every 750,000 years or so and smaller pieces of asteroid regularly make it through Earth's atmosphere. Once they have landed on the planet's surface, these rocks from space are called meteorites.

◀ FORMATION OF THE MOON

It is thought that the Moon formed after a massive asteroid hit the young Earth about 4.5 billion years ago. The Mars-sized asteroid gave Earth a glancing blow. Asteroid material and material expelled from Earth formed a massive cloud of gas, dust, and rock. Most of this eventually formed a doughnut-shaped ring around Earth. The pieces of ring material bumped and joined together as they orbited the planet until, finally, they produced one single, large body: the Moon.

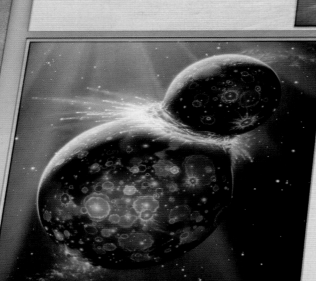

▼ ENDURANCE CRATER

There are tens of thousands of craters on Mars. Endurance Crater is 130 m (427 ft) wide and one of the best known. During 2004, the crater was photographed and examined by the rover *Opportunity*. Endurance is almost circular and bounded by a ring of rugged cliffs that slope down to the crater floor. Loose material and sand dunes cover the floor, making the crater shallower than when it formed.

Just beyond the crater, *Opportunity* came across the first meteorite to be discovered on another planet

◄ LUNAR CRATER

Daedalus Crater on the Moon is 58 miles (93 km) wide. Like other craters on the Moon that measure greater than about 6 miles (10 km) across, it has mountainous peaks at its centre. These formed as the land struck by the asteroid bounced back after the impact. At the same time, the crater's edge was pushed out and formed a circle of hills.

▼ CRATERED PLANET

Mercury is the most cratered planet. Most of its many millions of craters formed more than 3.5 billion years ago. They remain because the planet has no geological activity or weather to erode them away. They range in size from just a few feet across to one larger than the state of Texas.

Endurance Crater
427 ft (130 m)

▲ MANICOUAGAN CRATER

About 170 craters are known on Earth. The fifth largest is Manicouagan in Canada. It measures 62 miles (100 km) across and has changed since its formation about 214 million years ago. Rock has been eroded from the site, and water has filled the lower-lying ground and formed the Manicouagan Reservoir.

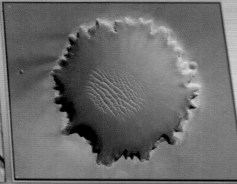

◄ VICTORIA CRATER

Many of the craters on Mars show signs of past erosion by wind and water. The scallop-shaped edge of the Victoria Crater formed as the crater's wall eroded and collapsed. Debris has filled the crater's floor, which is 0.5 miles (800 m) across, and a field of sand dunes has formed in the center.

VOLCANOES

The deeper you go into Earth's crust, the higher the temperature becomes. Below the solid crust is molten rock—magma. If there is a weak spot in the crust, or cracking caused by the movement of continental plates, the magma can rise up to the surface and spill out as lava. This is volcanism and it has occurred on all four rocky planets and many planetary moons, but as planets and moons cool, their crust thickens and volcanism eventually ceases. Volcanism stopped on the Moon about 3.5 billion years ago, but continues on Earth today.

❶ MAUNA LOA

Successive lava flows at one spot can build up to form a volcano. Most of Earth's volcanoes occur at the edges of its continental plates. Mauna Loa is one of a chain of active and inactive volcanic islands produced where the Pacific plate moves over a hot spot in Earth's mantle. The volcanoes here are shield-shaped, with broad bases and shallow slopes. They grew through gentle eruptions of runny lava that erupts up to 1,312 ft (400 m) into the air.

❷ VESUVIUS

When one of Earth's continental plates is forced under another, there is frictional heating, which can lead to volcanism. Mount Vesuvius near Naples, Italy, was produced in this way. Volcanoes like Vesuvius do not erupt very often, but when they do the effect is devastating. A towering cloud of ash and pumice is ejected from the caldera, and tsunamis are generated in the nearby sea.

A fire fountain of lava leaps into the air

❸ OLYMPUS MONS

Towering 15 miles (24 km) above the surrounding land, and with a base width of 600 km (373 miles), the volcano Olympus Mons is a global landmark on Mars. At three times the height of Earth's Mount Everest, it is the tallest mountain in the solar system. This bird's-eye view shows the caldera at its peak, which was produced by the collapse of the underlying chamber that once contained magma.

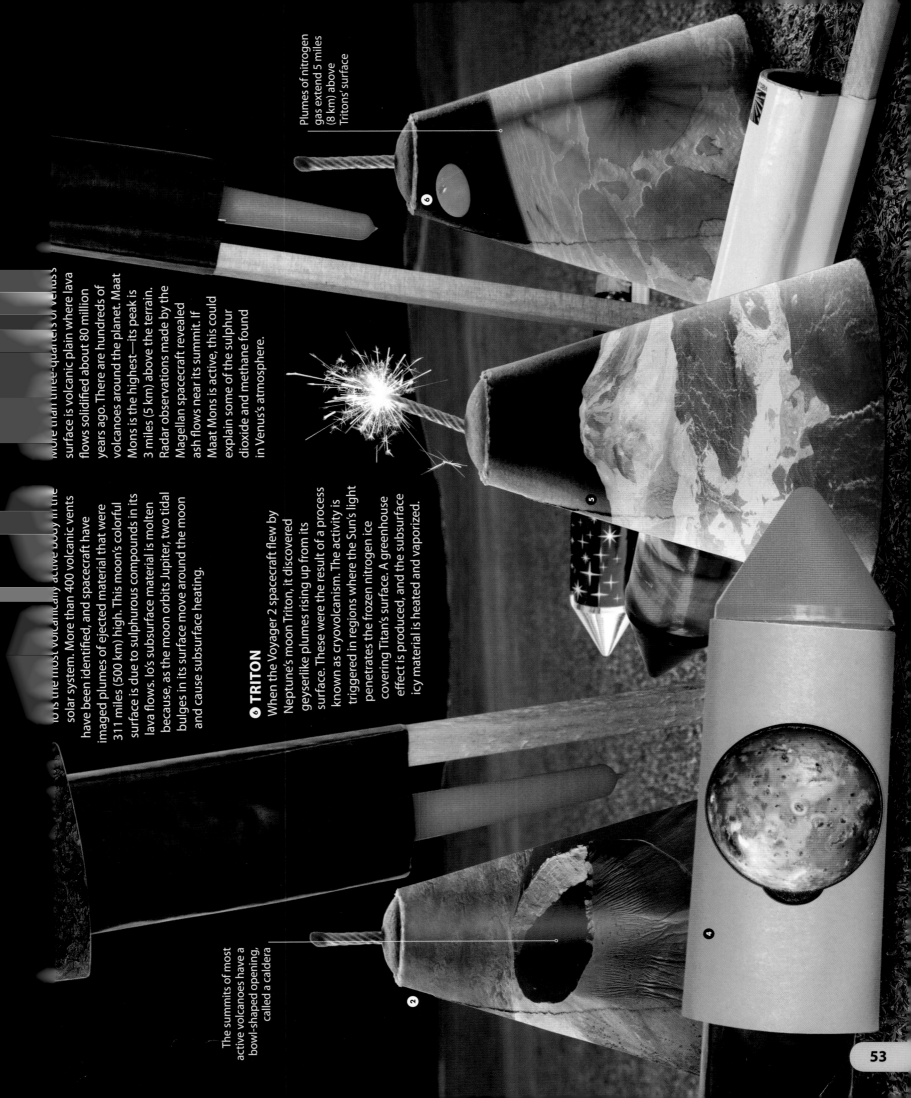

Plumes of nitrogen gas extend 5 miles (8 km) above Triton's surface

...more than three-quarters of Venus's surface is volcanic plain where lava flows solidified about 80 million years ago. There are hundreds of volcanoes around the planet. Maat Mons is the highest—its peak is 3 miles (5 km) above the terrain. Radar observations made by the Magellan spacecraft revealed ash flows near its summit. If Maat Mons is active, this could explain some of the sulphur dioxide and methane found in Venus's atmosphere.

Io is the most volcanically active body in the solar system. More than 400 volcanic vents have been identified, and spacecraft have imaged plumes of ejected material that were 311 miles (500 km) high. This moon's colorful surface is due to sulphurous compounds in its lava flows. Io's subsurface material is molten because, as the moon orbits Jupiter, two tidal bulges in its surface move around the moon and cause subsurface heating.

⑥ TRITON

When the Voyager 2 spacecraft flew by Neptune's moon Triton, it discovered geyserlike plumes rising up from its surface. These were the result of a process known as cryovolcanism. The activity is triggered in regions where the Sun's light penetrates the frozen nitrogen ice covering Titan's surface. A greenhouse effect is produced, and the subsurface icy material is heated and vaporized.

The summits of most active volcanoes have a bowl-shaped opening, called a caldera.

WATER

Water is familiar to us on Earth; it dominates our planet's surface and it is essential to life on the planet—without it we would not exist. Water is found on Earth in its liquid form, its solid state, and as a gas. It has been discovered elsewhere in the solar system, but not in such abundance and only in its frozen and gaseous states. Jupiter has gaseous water clouds, and comets are two-thirds water in the form of snow and ice.

❶ Water world Most of Earth's water is liquid and most of this is in its oceans, which cover more than 70 percent of the planet's surface. About two percent is in ice sheets and glaciers, and less than one percent in rivers, lakes, and the atmosphere. Even so, water is not common. If Earth's surface were smooth, the oceans would be just 1.7 miles (2.8 km) deep.

❷ Ice on Mars Water exists as ice or vapour on the planet Mars. The planet's southern polar cap consists of mostly water ice roughly centered on the planet's south pole. The polar cap's swirling pattern is surrounded by hundreds of square miles of permafrost— water ice mixed into the soil that is frozen to the hardness of solid rock.

❸ Watery past When Mars was young, some 3–4 billion years ago, it was warmer and had liquid water. This flowed across the surface, carving out valleys and forming lakes and seas. Echus Chasma is 62 miles (100 km) long and was formed when flowing ground water cut through surface rock. The water, now frozen in the planet's surface layer, could flow again if changes in Mars's orbit trigger global melting.

❹ Hidden ocean Europa is the fourth largest of Jupiter's moons and a little smaller than Earth's Moon. It is a ball of rock with a water-ice surface that is tens of miles thick. A liquid water layer that may contain more water than Earth's oceans combined is thought to exist below the ice. Europa's liquid sea may be a haven for life.

❺ Water and life Liquid water was essential for the development of life on Earth. Once the young Earth had cooled enough for water to be liquid on its surface, life broke out. About 3.8 billion years ago, carbon-containing molecules evolved into living cells in its oceans. Over time, these evolved into ever more complex creatures. About 450 million years ago, some of these moved from the water to the land.

MOON

The Moon is a dead, dry, desolate place. It is about a quarter of Earth's width and made of about one-eightieth of the amount of material that Earth has. This means this rocky world is not able to hold on to a significant atmosphere, and its interior is too cold for any geological activity to take place. The lighter-colored regions visible from Earth are mountains formed by asteroid impacts, and the dark areas, known as maria, are vast fields of solidified lava that flowed onto the surface about 3.6 billion years ago.

▼ LUNAR SOIL

A soil-like blanket several feet thick covers most of the Moon. On the surface it is fine-grained, but the particle size gets progressively bigger farther down. Solid rock is reached about 16.4 feet (5 m) down on the maria, and the soil is 32.8 feet (10 m) deep in the mountainous regions. The soil was produced by asteroids smashing into the surface at around 12.4 miles (20 km) per second. The rock was pulverized and craters produced.

SURFACE FEATURES ▶

The lunar surface was shaped when the Moon was young. A few billion years of persistent asteroid bombardments were followed by volcanic lava welling up from the Moon's interior and filling low-lying regions. Visible here is the smooth, dark basaltic lava of Mare Imbrium (lower left), which contrasts with the lighter, older highland rock. On Mare Imbrium's northern rim is Plato, one of thousands of craters on the Moon.

The huge boulder called Split Rock rolled into this valley after being blasted from a crater in Mare Serenitatis

The Lunar Roving Vehicle transported astronaut Harrison Schmitt and the rock and soil samples he collected

JULY

PHASE CYCLE ▶

The Moon rotates once in the same time it takes to make one orbit of Earth and so keeps the same face always pointing towards us. As it orbits, its face appears to change shape because sunlight falls on different portions of it. As the Moon orbits, the sunlit portion diminishes, then grows. When on the opposite side of Earth to the Sun, it is fully lit—the full Moon. These changes in appearance are called phases and a complete cycle of phases takes 29.5 days.

SUNDAY	MONDAY	TUESDAY	WEDNESDAY	THURSDAY	FRIDAY	SATURDAY
1	2	3	4	5	6	7
8	9	10	11	12	13	14
15	16	17	18	19	20	21
22	23	24	25	26	27	28
29	30	31				

LUNAR MYTHS ◀

Throughout history, some people have thought that humans are affected by the Moon. Our word "lunatic" (from *luna*, the Latin for Moon) comes from the belief that the full Moon turns people mad. Myths and stories tell of humans changing into violent, wolflike creatures during a full Moon. Even today, many people believe that the full Moon can affect human behavior. However, sound statistical analysis shows there is no lunar effect.

TIDES ON EARTH ▶

The gravity of the Moon and the Sun pull on the surface waters of Earth and this produces tides. At a normal seaside resort there are two high tides and two low tides a day, and the timing of the tides changes according to the position of the Moon in the sky. The height of the tides is also affected by the phase of the Moon—when there is a new or full Moon, for example, the tides are particularly high.

ECLIPSES

The Sun and Moon are vastly different sizes, but they appear the same size in Earth's sky. Even though the Moon is 400 times smaller than the Sun, it is also about 400 times closer. This means that, whenever the Moon passes directly in front of the Sun, it covers the Sun's face. At totality, when the Sun's face is completely covered, most of its sunlight is blocked from reaching Earth. At other times, the Moon passes into the Earth's shadow and is eclipsed.

Brass sphere represents the Sun

▶ SOLAR ECLIPSE
There are about 75 total solar eclipses every 100 years. These occur when the Sun's face is totally covered by the Moon. During this brief time, the Sun's corona becomes visible. The maximum length of totality is 7.6 minutes. The shadow cast by the Moon falls on Earth. Anyone within the inner shadow sees the total eclipse, while those in its outer part see the Sun's disk only partially covered by the Moon—a partial eclipse.

◀ SHADOW ON THE EARTH
The dark smudge in the center of the picture is the shadow cast by the Moon on Earth during the total solar eclipse of August 11, 1999. At its widest, the shadow measured 135 miles (217 km) across, and it moved eastwards at about 1,056 mph (1,700 kph). Eclipses occur in the same place on average once every 375 years.

The papier-mâché Earth spins as it orbits the Sun

▲ VIEWING AN ECLIPSE

A safe way to observe a solar eclipse is by projecting an image of the Sun onto a piece of card. The eclipse starts as the disk of the Moon begins to encroach on the face of the Sun. The Sun is progressively hidden until it is completely covered during totality—from first contact to totality takes about one hour. Only in the last few minutes before totality does the light dim significantly.

The side of the Moon facing the Sun receives light

▲ RINGS AND BEADS

At the beginning and end of totality, small portions of the solar disk can be glimpsed through valleys and depressions on the Moon. The effect from Earth is an apparent set of luminous beads strung around the dark Moon. For a second or two, the scene can be transformed into a huge, sparkling diamond ring as light floods through a gap.

◀ ORRERY

An orrery is a model used to demonstrate the movement of planetary bodies around the Sun. The one shown here, which is not to scale, indicates how both Earth and the Moon can cast shadows and how these can lead to eclipses. It also illustrates how the distance between Earth and the Sun varies during the year, and how the year divides into months as the Moon orbits Earth.

▶ ECLIPSE MYTHS

Throughout history, many cultures have thought of solar eclipses as omens of disasters. Chinese people thought an invisible dragon was swallowing the Sun. By drumming and banging on pans, the dragon was frightened into regurgitating the Sun, and daylight was restored.

In Buddhist legend, Rahu is thought to cause eclipses by swallowing the Sun

▲ RED MOON

Lunar eclipses occur about twice a year. They happen when the Sun, Earth, and Moon are aligned and the Moon passes through the shadow cast by Earth. For just over an hour, the Moon turns a dull red color as sunlight is scattered by molecules and dust in Earth's upper atmosphere.

ASTEROIDS

Most of the billions of asteroids that orbit the Sun do so in the Main Belt between Mars and Jupiter. They are pieces of material that failed to form a planet in this part of the solar system because Jupiter's gravity prevented the bits combining to create a single object. Asteroids outside the belt include two groups that move along Jupiter's orbit and are known as the Trojans, and the near-Earth asteroids whose orbits bring them closer to Earth.

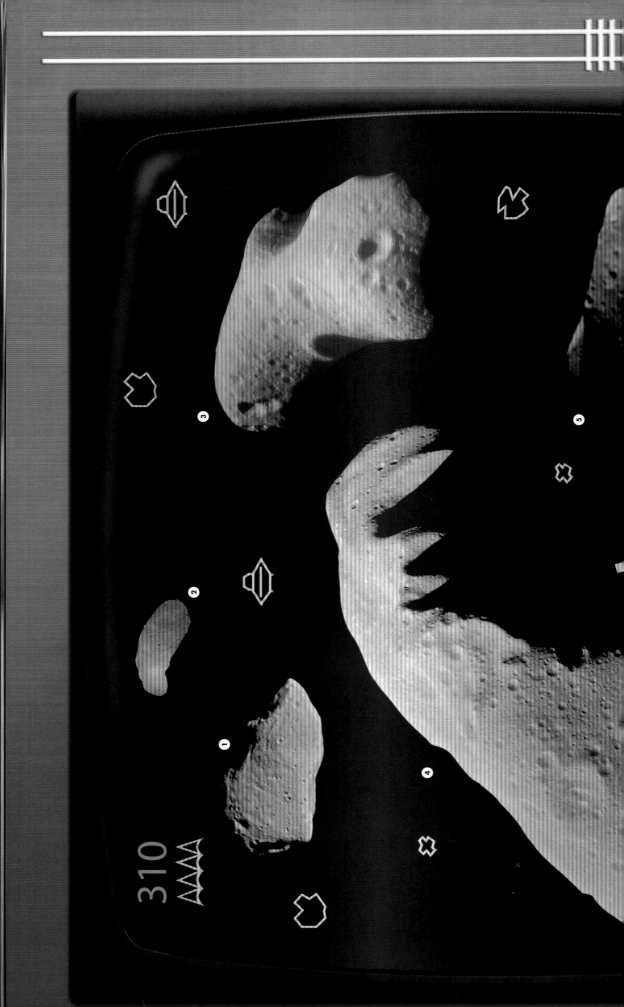

310

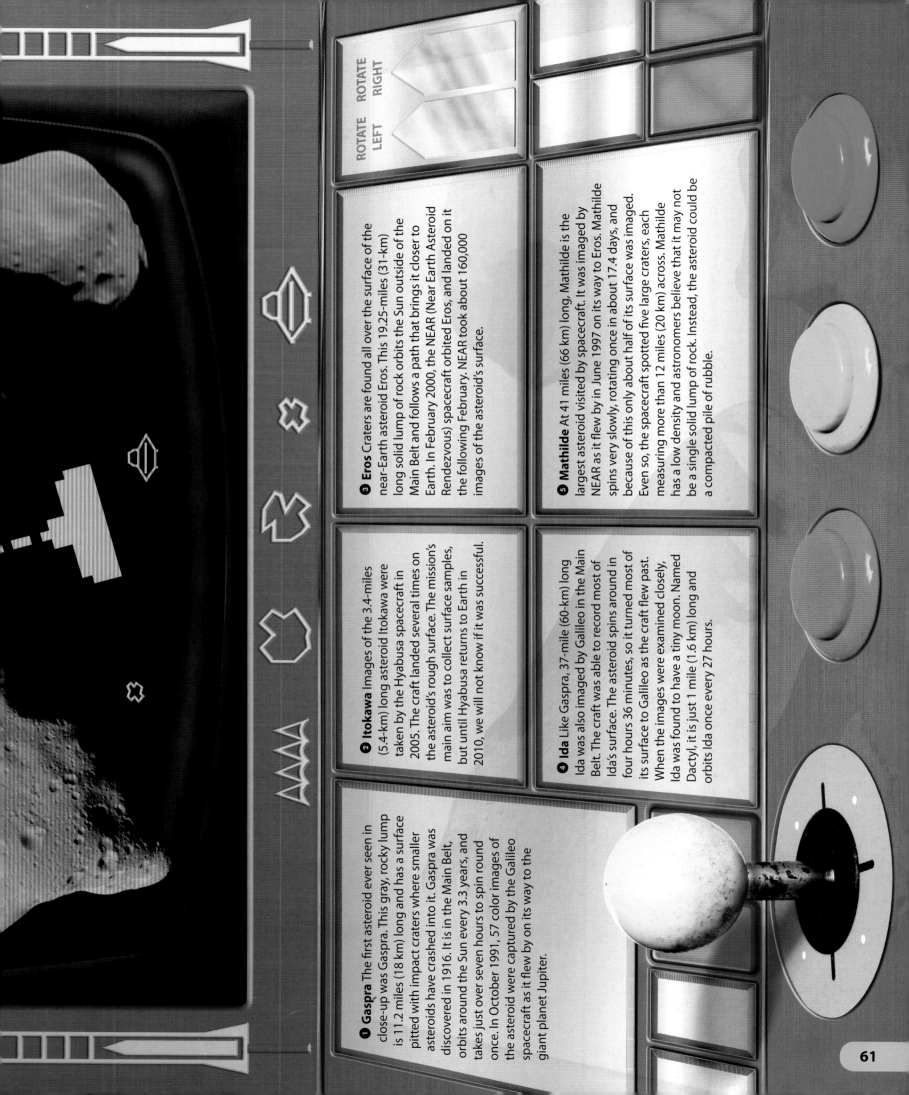

❶ Gaspra The first asteroid ever seen in close-up was Gaspra. This gray, rocky lump is 11.2 miles (18 km) long and has a surface pitted with impact craters where smaller asteroids have crashed into it. Gaspra was discovered in 1916. It is in the Main Belt, orbits around the Sun every 3.3 years, and takes just over seven hours to spin round once. In October 1991, 57 color images of the asteroid were captured by the Galileo spacecraft as it flew by on its way to the giant planet Jupiter.

❷ Itokawa Images of the 3.4-miles (5.4-km) long asteroid Itokawa were taken by the Hyabusa spacecraft in 2005. The craft landed several times on the asteroid's rough surface. The mission's main aim was to collect surface samples, but until Hyabusa returns to Earth in 2010, we will not know if it was successful.

❸ Eros Craters are found all over the surface of the near-Earth asteroid Eros. This 19.25-miles (31-km) long solid lump of rock orbits the Sun outside of the Main Belt and follows a path that brings it closer to Earth. In February 2000, the NEAR (Near Earth Asteroid Rendezvous) spacecraft orbited Eros, and landed on it the following February. NEAR took about 160,000 images of the asteroid's surface.

❹ Ida Like Gaspra, 37-mile (60-km) long Ida was also imaged by Galileo in the Main Belt. The craft was able to record most of Ida's surface. The asteroid spins around in four hours 36 minutes, so it turned most of its surface to Galileo as the craft flew past. When the images were examined closely, Ida was found to have a tiny moon. Named Dactyl, it is just 1 mile (1.6 km) long and orbits Ida once every 27 hours.

❺ Mathilde At 41 miles (66 km) long, Mathilde is the largest asteroid visited by spacecraft. It was imaged by NEAR as it flew by in June 1997 on its way to Eros. Mathilde spins very slowly, rotating once in about 17.4 days, and because of this only about half of its surface was imaged. Even so, the spacecraft spotted five large craters, each measuring more than 12 miles (20 km) across. Mathilde has a low density and astronomers believe that it may not be a single solid lump of rock. Instead, the asteroid could be a compacted pile of rubble.

GIANT PLANETS

Jupiter, Saturn, Uranus, and Neptune are giant-sized worlds that orbit the Sun far beyond Earth. They are ice-cold planets, each with a system of rings around it and a large family of moons. When we look at these giants, we see layers of clouds in a deep gas atmosphere that merges into liquid underneath. Jupiter and Saturn have been known of since ancient times, while Uranus and Neptune were discovered more recently by telescope.

JUPITER ▶

Huge Jupiter, the largest of all the solar system planets, is named after the king of the Roman gods and ruler of the heavens. It is also the most massive planet: It is made of 2.5 times the material of the other seven planets combined. However, its great size means its density is low—it is only 318 times the mass of Earth, yet 1,300 Earths would fit inside it.

▲ SATURN

All four giants are oblate in shape and Saturn is the most oblate of all. This means that they are all wider round their equators than around the poles. Saturn is a fast spinner—it completes an entire rotation every 10.7 hours. As it spins, material is flung outward, giving the planet a bulging equator. Saturn is also the least dense planet: If placed in a vast ocean of water, it would float.

GIANT STRUCTURE ▶

Jupiter and Saturn are made mainly of hydrogen and helium, with small amounts of other elements. Within their atmospheres this material is in the form of gas. Underneath, the material's density and temperature alter with depth, and the physical state of the material changes. Below Jupiter's gas atmosphere, its hydrogen becomes more like a liquid. Deeper still, it is like a molten metal.

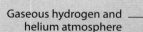
Gaseous hydrogen and helium atmosphere

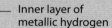
Inner layer of metallic hydrogen

Core of rock, metal, and hydrogen compounds

Outer layer of liquid hydrogen and helium

HERSCHEL ▶

On March 13, 1781, astronomer William Herschel was looking at the night sky when he observed something that he at first took to be a comet. It was the planet Uranus. The six planets from Mercury to Saturn had been known of since the first humans studied the sky. Uranus was the first planet to actually be discovered, and its distance from the Sun doubled the size of the known solar system overnight.

◀ GALLE

Neptune was discovered by Johann Galle on September 23, 1846 after its location in the sky had been predicted. Astronomers observing Uranus saw that it was not moving exactly as expected along its orbit. They thought a more distant planet was disturbing it. The postion of this possible planet was calculated and on the first night of his search Galle discovered Neptune.

▼ NEPTUNE

Neptune orbits the Sun about 30 times more distant than Earth. Anyone so far from the Sun would see it appear 900 times dimmer than on Earth. They would also miss the Sun's heat—Neptune's cloud-top temperature is an icy -320°F (-200°C). Neptune is similar in size and internal structure to Uranus, and its blue coloring is also the result of methane absorbing red light.

◀ URANUS

At four times the size of Earth, Uranus is the third-largest planet. Like the other giants, it doesn't have a solid surface. Layers of methane ice cloud in its hydrogen-rich atmosphere form its visible surface. Methane gas within the atmosphere absorbs the red wavelengths in sunlight, making the planet appear blue. Beneath its atmosphere is a layer of water, methane, and ammonia. At its heart is a core of rock.

STORMY WEATHER

All four giant planets are stormy places. Their upper atmospheres blow around in bands parallel to their equators. Here gas is channeled around the planets at high speed, and clouds and storms take shape. The storms on colorful Jupiter are easy to see. These white and dark spots stand out against the planet's banded upper atmosphere. Those of Saturn, Uranus, and Neptune are not so obvious. Their visible surfaces may look calm, but fierce winds and storms rage on them, too.

❶ GREAT RED SPOT

Jupiter's storms are huge. The smallest are the size of the largest hurricanes on Earth, while the biggest, the Great Red Spot, is bigger than Earth itself. It rotates anticlockwise every six to seven days. Unlike the smaller storms, which last only days, the Great Red Spot has been seen for more than 300 years. A smaller version, called Red Spot Jnr., emerged close by in 2000.

❷ BANDED APPEARANCE

Jupiter's upper atmosphere is shown here unfurled to reveal the bands that surround the planet. The white bands are cool rising gas and are known as zones. The red-brown bands are warmer gas and are known as belts. The atmosphere is mainly hydrogen with helium, but it is other chemical compounds that provide the color as they form clouds at different altitudes.

❸ DRAGON STORM

A giant thunderstorm glows pale orange in this false-color image of Saturn. Named the Dragon Storm, it raged in a region nicknamed Storm Alley, because of its many storms witnessed during 2004. Saturn's atmosphere is full of storms and winds, but Storm Alley, located in the planet's southern hemisphere, is unusual. It is one of the few places on Saturn where the winds blow to the west.

❹ GREAT DARK SPOT

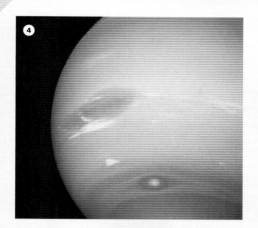

When Voyager 2 flew by Neptune in 1989, it revealed a huge, dark storm in the planet's southern hemisphere. Known as the Great Dark Spot and about the size of Earth, the storm was accompanied by bright high-altitude clouds. Winds near the storm blew at up to 1,500 mph (2,400 kph), the strongest in the solar system. By 1994, the storm had disappeared, but another, the Northern Great Dark Spot, had appeared in Neptune's northern hemisphere.

❺ CLOUDS OF URANUS

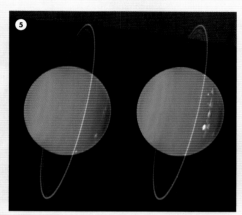

By looking at Uranus in infrared light, we peer through the haze that surrounds the planet and makes it look featureless, and see the clouds below. The highest clouds appear white, the middle-level ones are bright blue, and the lowest clouds are dark blue. The clouds are thought to change with Uranus's extreme seasons. Due to its tilt, each of Uranus's poles points to the Sun for 21 years at a time.

❻ SATURN'S AURORAE

Electric blue lights dance near Saturn's South Pole. The light display is an aurora—a phenomenon regularly witnessed in Earth's polar regions. Unlike Earth's aurorae, which last for minutes or hours and are seen in visible light, those on Saturn can last several days and are only visible in the ultraviolet. The aurorae are triggered by particles from the Sun, known as the solar wind, interacting with the planet's upper atmosphere.

RINGS

Huge rings of material encircle the four largest planets, extending out beyond each planet's equatorial region. Only Saturn's rings are easily visible from Earth, but spacecraft have provided close-up views of all four ring systems. The rings appear solid, but are made of individual pieces of material that follow their own orbits around their planet. Saturn's is the most extensive ring system and was the first to be discovered.

▼ URANUS'S RINGS

The second planet discovered to have rings was Uranus. The first five of its 11 rings were discovered in 1977. Astronomers were observing the passage of a star behind the planet and noticed it blink on and off when near Uranus as its light was blocked by the rings. The individual rings are narrow and widely separated, and the whole system is more gap than ring.

▼ JUPITER'S RINGS

The two pale orange lines seen here beyond the blue-colored edge of Jupiter are the planet's thin main ring. The lower line is the ring at the far side of the planet. The part nearest Jupiter is hidden from view by Jupiter's shadow. The main ring is about 4,350 miles (7,000 km) wide and less than 18 miles (30 km) deep. Out of view, and at either side of the main ring, are the almost cloudlike halo and gossamer rings.

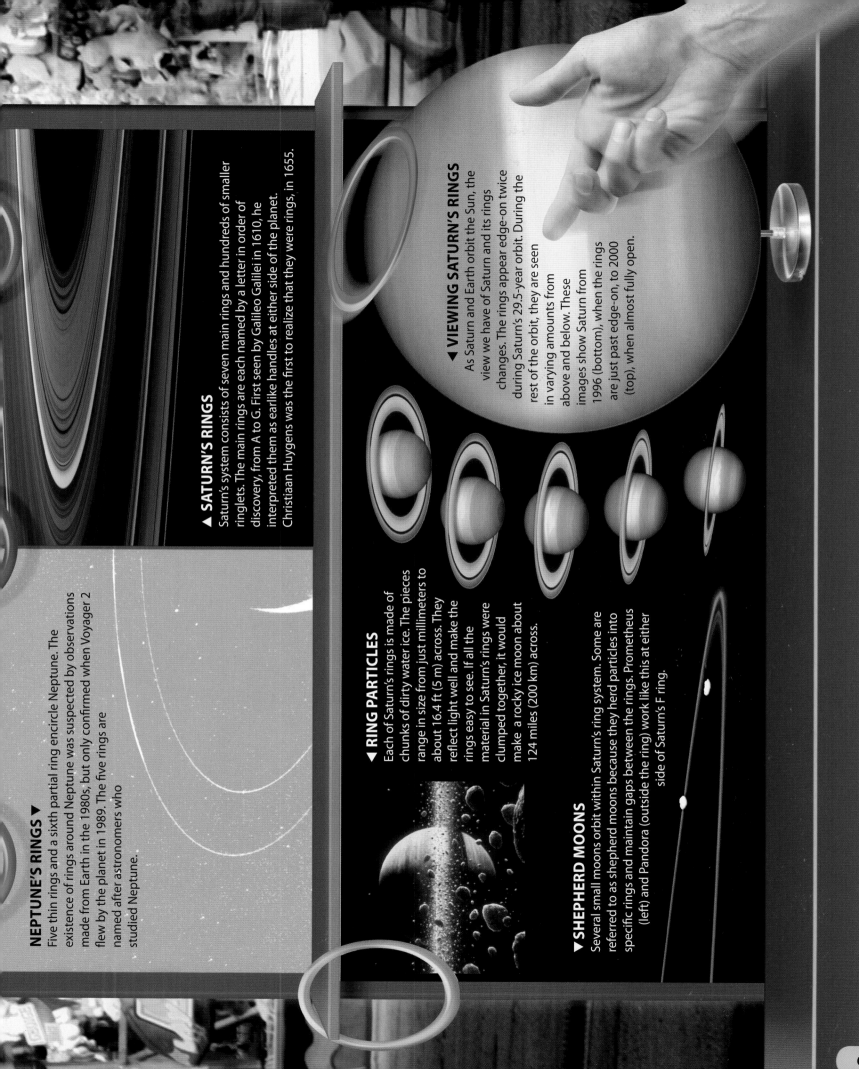

NEPTUNE'S RINGS ▼

Five thin rings and a sixth partial ring encircle Neptune. The existence of rings around Neptune was suspected by observations made from Earth in the 1980s, but only confirmed when Voyager 2 flew by the planet in 1989. The five rings are named after astronomers who studied Neptune.

▲ SATURN'S RINGS

Saturn's system consists of seven main rings and hundreds of smaller ringlets. The main rings are each named by a letter in order of discovery, from A to G. First seen by Galileo Galilei in 1610, he interpreted them as earlike handles at either side of the planet. Christiaan Huygens was the first to realize that they were rings, in 1655.

▲ RING PARTICLES

Each of Saturn's rings is made of chunks of dirty water ice. The pieces range in size from just millimeters to about 16.4 ft (5 m) across. They reflect light well and make the rings easy to see. If all the material in Saturn's rings were clumped together, it would make a rocky ice moon about 124 miles (200 km) across.

▼ SHEPHERD MOONS

Several small moons orbit within Saturn's ring system. Some are referred to as shepherd moons because they herd particles into specific rings and maintain gaps between the rings. Prometheus (left) and Pandora (outside the ring) work like this at either side of Saturn's F ring.

▲ VIEWING SATURN'S RINGS

As Saturn and Earth orbit the Sun, the view we have of Saturn and its rings changes. The rings appear edge-on twice during Saturn's 29.5-year orbit. During the rest of the orbit, they are seen in varying amounts from above and below. These images show Saturn from 1996 (bottom), when the rings are just past edge-on, to 2000 (top), when almost fully open.

BEYOND NEPTUNE

Billions of miles away from the Sun, in the dark outer region of the solar system, are trillions of ice-cold worlds. Much smaller than the planets, the largest objects in this region are the dwarf planets Eris and Pluto, which orbit among the Kuiper Belt objects. We know little about any of these worlds. The first spacecraft to explore this region will be New Horizons when it arrives in 2015. More distant and more numerous are the smaller comets that make up the Oort Cloud.

❶ KUIPER BELT

The Kuiper Belt is a flattened ring-shaped region of space occupied by mainly irregular-shaped bodies made of ice and rock. The first Kuiper Belt object was discovered in 1992. So far, about a thousand have been identified, but tens of thousands more are believed to exist. The larger members of the belt are classified as dwarf planets. The belt also contains some comets.

❷ ERIS

The discovery of Eris in 2005 shook up astronomers' thinking about the outer part of the solar system. It was found to be larger than Pluto, which was then thought of as the ninth planet. It was decided to introduce a new class of object: the dwarf planet—an almost round body that orbits the Sun in the neighborhood of other orbiting bodies. Eris takes 560 years to complete its orbit and has one moon, Dysnomia.

Uranus's orbit

Pluto's orbit

Neptune's orbit

Kuiper Belt

❸ MAKEMAKE AND HAUMEA

Red-colored Makemake and the egg-shaped Haumea are the third- and fourth-largest dwarf planets. The two are also known as plutoids. The term plutoids was introduced in 2008 and is used for the dwarf planets in the Kuiper Belt. In this way, they are distinguished from dwarf planets that exist outside the Kuiper Belt. Just one is known at present, the largest asteroid, Ceres.

❹ PLUTO

Pluto was classed as a planet from its discovery in 1930 until 2006. It is 1,432 miles (2,304 km) across and has a surface temperature of about -380°F (-230°C). Pluto has three moons. The largest, Charon, has been known of since 1978. Hydra and Nix were discovered in 2005 in images taken by the Hubble Space Telescope.

❺ GERARD KUIPER

The Kuiper Belt is named after Dutch-American astronomer Gerard Kuiper. In 1951, he suggested that those comets that make repeat journeys through the solar system at regular intervals started off from a region of rock and ice bodies just beyond Neptune. Kuiper also discovered two planetary moons—Uranus's Miranda and Neptune's Nereid.

Oort Cloud   Kuiper Belt   Comet orbit

❻ OORT CLOUD

Surrounding the disk-shaped planetary part of the solar system is the Oort Cloud, a vast sphere of comets. They are the leftover material from when the planets formed. The comets don't orbit in the same plane as the planets and follow elongated paths around the Sun. The outer edge of the cloud is about 1.6 light-years away, nearly halfway to the nearest stars. Occasionally, comets leave the cloud and move into the inner solar system.

MOONS

Six of the solar system planets share more than 160 moons between them. Earth has just one, the Moon, but Jupiter and Saturn have more than 60 each. The moons vary greatly in size and in distance from their planet; each one follows its own orbit. The moons are made of mainly rock, or of mainly rock and ice. The largest is Ganymede. Another 18 are more than 250 miles (400 km) wide. All of these are roughly spherical in shape, but the more numerous, smaller moons are irregular.

❶ **The Moon** Earth's Moon is about a quarter of the Earth's size and the fifth largest of all the moons. It is a lifeless ball of mainly rock that orbits Earth every 27.3 days. Its surface is covered by craters, many of which were flooded by volcanic lava more than three billion years ago.

❷ **Phobos** Mars has two moons. The largest is Phobos, a potato-shaped rocky body that measures 16.6 miles (26.8 km) long and orbits Mars in just over 7.6 hours. Along with Deimos, it is thought to be an asteroid that was captured into orbit around Mars early in the planet's history.

❸ **Callisto** Callisto is one of the four Galilean moons; they are named after the astronomer Galileo Galilei who discovered them. The others are Ganymede, Europa, and Io. White patches on Callisto's surface are the icy floors of its impact craters, which were formed when asteroids collided into the moon.

❹ **Ganymede** The largest moon of Jupiter, Ganymede is also the biggest moon in the solar system. It is larger than Mercury and about three-quarters the size of Mars. It is a rock and ice world that measures 3,267 miles (5,262 km) across and orbits the planet in just over seven days.

❺ **Europa** Europa is the smallest of Jupiter's Galilean moons, with a diameter that measures 1,939 miles (3,122 km) across. Its ice-covered surface is one of the smoothest in the solar system and it is streaked with dark lines where fresh ice has erupted into surface cracks.

❻ **Io** Highly colored Io is just a little larger than Earth's Moon. It orbits Jupiter every 1.7 days at a distance only slightly greater than the Moon is from Earth. Io is unlike the other Galilean moons and any other planetary moon. Its surface has active volcanoes and is covered by lava flows.

Deimos

EARTH

MARS

JUPITER

▼ ORIGINS

Most of the large moons are believed to have formed from material unused in the planet-making process, and at about the same time as their planet. Unusually, the Moon is made largely of material knocked out of Earth when an asteroid collided with the planet. The largest moons are worlds in their own right with surfaces that have changed due to forces such as volcanism. Many of the smaller ones, including Mars's two moons, Phobos and Deimos, were originally asteroids.

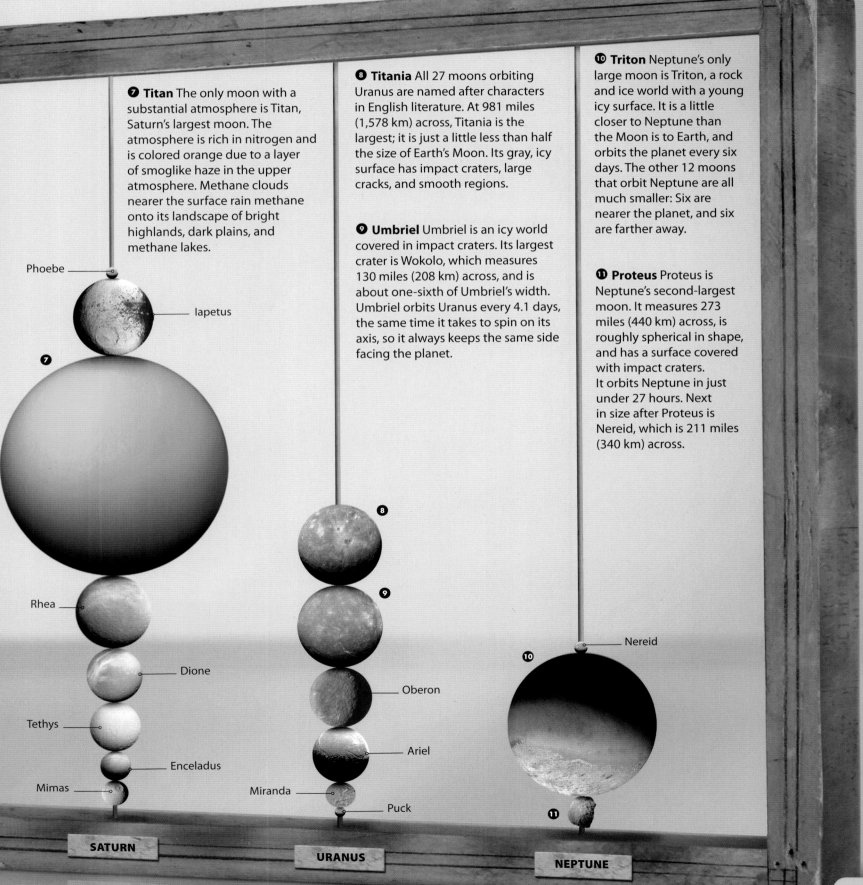

❼ Titan The only moon with a substantial atmosphere is Titan, Saturn's largest moon. The atmosphere is rich in nitrogen and is colored orange due to a layer of smoglike haze in the upper atmosphere. Methane clouds nearer the surface rain methane onto its landscape of bright highlands, dark plains, and methane lakes.

❽ Titania All 27 moons orbiting Uranus are named after characters in English literature. At 981 miles (1,578 km) across, Titania is the largest; it is just a little less than half the size of Earth's Moon. Its gray, icy surface has impact craters, large cracks, and smooth regions.

❾ Umbriel Umbriel is an icy world covered in impact craters. Its largest crater is Wokolo, which measures 130 miles (208 km) across, and is about one-sixth of Umbriel's width. Umbriel orbits Uranus every 4.1 days, the same time it takes to spin on its axis, so it always keeps the same side facing the planet.

❿ Triton Neptune's only large moon is Triton, a rock and ice world with a young icy surface. It is a little closer to Neptune than the Moon is to Earth, and orbits the planet every six days. The other 12 moons that orbit Neptune are all much smaller: Six are nearer the planet, and six are farther away.

⓫ Proteus Proteus is Neptune's second-largest moon. It measures 273 miles (440 km) across, is roughly spherical in shape, and has a surface covered with impact craters. It orbits Neptune in just under 27 hours. Next in size after Proteus is Nereid, which is 211 miles (340 km) across.

Phoebe

Iapetus

Rhea

Dione

Tethys

Enceladus

Mimas

Oberon

Ariel

Miranda

Puck

Nereid

SATURN

URANUS

NEPTUNE

71

COMETS

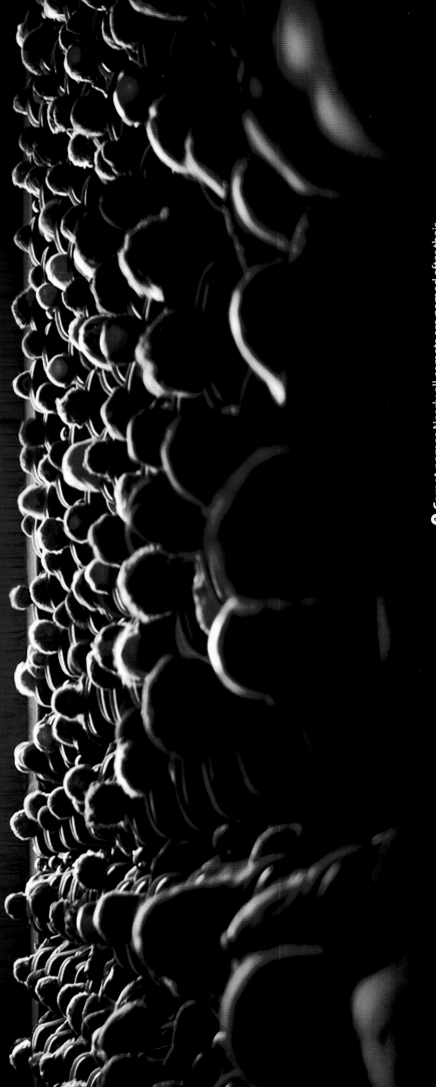

Far beyond the planets there are trillions of comets. Each is a huge dirty snowball which follows its own long orbit around the Sun. Most belong to the Oort Cloud, a distant sphere of comets surrounding the rest of the solar system. Others come from the Kuiper Belt. Every so often, one of these dirty snowballs is knocked onto a new orbit that takes it in towards the Sun. As it approaches the Sun, it undergoes a dramatic change in size and appearance.

❶ Nucleus The huge dirty snowball is called a comet nucleus. It is a mix of two-thirds snow and one-third silicate-rock dust. Irregular in shape and about the size of a big city, a nucleus is usually too distant to be seen. A few have been imaged by spacecraft. These views of the 3.4-miles (5.5-km) long Wild 2 nucleus were taken by Stardust in 2004.

❷ Changing comet When a comet nucleus approaches the Sun, its surface snow turns to gas, and dust is loosened in the process. A huge head, called a coma, and two tails form, one made from gas, the other from dust. They grow as the comet (shown here from left to right) nears the Sun, then they stop growing and appear to shrink as it moves away.

❸ Comet names Nearly all comets are named after their discoverer. If two or three people discover the comet independently, all their names are used. Halley's Comet is an exception to this rule. This comet was first seen hundreds of years ago, but it takes its name from Edmond Halley, who calculated that comets periodically return to Earth's sky as they orbit the Sun. He correctly predicted the return of the comet that now bears his name.

❹ Comet tails A comet forms two tails from the gas and dust released from its nucleus. They are usually millions of miles long and make the comet easy to see. Comet West was visible by the naked eye in Earth's sky in 1976. A comet's gas tail is blue and straight and its dust tail is white and curves out away from the nucleus.

❺ Discovery There are more than 50 comets with the name McNaught because each was discovered by Robert McNaught. No person has discovered more, although more than 1,600 have been found in the SOHO spacecraft data. This Comet McNaught was discovered on August 7, 2006 and was easily seen in early 2007.

❻ Great comets Comet Hyakutake was discovered by Yuji Hyakutake using a pair of high-powered binoculars in 1996. Its gas tail was 355 million miles (570 million km) long, the longest ever detected. The comet will return in about 30,000 years. A particularly spectacular comet is seen in Earth's sky three or four times a century.

❼ End of a comet A comet travelling in the inner solar system doesn't last forever. Its nucleus gets smaller on each orbit as its material is used to form a coma and tails. Some comets pass too close to Jupiter and are affected by its gravity. Comet Shoemaker-Levy 9 was pulled apart and its pieces crashed into the planet in July 1994.

METEORITES

Meteorites are pieces of spacerock that have traveled through Earth's atmosphere and landed on its surface. About 3,000 meteorites weighing more than 2 lb (1 kg) each land on Earth every year. Most fall into the oceans and are never found. Those that fall on the land can be found by chance or as part of an organized search. Most meteorites are pieces of asteroid.

STONY METEORITE ▲

More than 30,000 meteorites have been collected and catalogued. They are classified according to three main types: stony, stony-iron, and iron. The stony meteorites are composed mostly of silicate rock and are the most common.

▲ MARTIAN ORIGIN

More than 30 of the meteorites found on Earth traveled here from Mars. These chunks of Martian rock were blasted off the planet when asteroids hit it. We know they come from Mars because they contain small amounts of gas that are similar to those found in the Martian atmosphere.

◄ STONY-IRON METEORITE

Meteorites made up of roughly equal amounts of nickel-iron and silicate rock are classified as stony-irons. They are the rarest group and make up a very small percentage of the weight of all known meteorites.

IRON METEORITE ▲

Iron meteorites consist of mainly iron and nickel and are the second most common type. They are usually bigger than the stony or stony-iron meteorites because they lose less material as they travel through Earth's atmosphere.

◄ NAMING METEORITES

Meteorites are named after the place where they fell or are found. The Sikhote Alin is one of a number that bear this name. The fragments are the remains of an iron asteroid that broke up in Earth's atmosphere and fell as a shower in the Sikhote Alin mountain range of Siberia on February 12, 1947.

▶ FALLS AND FINDS

Some meteorites are seen to fall to Earth and these are referred to as "falls." Most, however, arrive unnoticed and when these are discovered they are called "finds." This iron meteorite is one of many called Gibeon that have been found in a region near the town of Gibeon in Namibia since the 1830s.

METEOR ▼

Tiny fragments of asteroid or comet that travel through Earth's atmosphere can produce meteors. These are short-lived trails of light seen in Earth's night sky. The fragment produces a trail of excited atoms which in turn produce light. The meteors last for less than a second and are popularly known as shooting stars.

▲ LUNAR METEORITE

More than 60 meteorites found so far on Earth originated on the Moon. This one was found in Antarctica, where dark meteorites are easy to spot on the virtually rock-free white landscape. It was found in 1981 and was the first meteorite to be identified as coming from the Moon.

METEORITE SHOWER ▲

The stony Nakhla meteorite originated on Mars. It was seen to land in Egypt on June 28, 1911 as part of a shower of stones—the result of one large body breaking up in Earth's atmosphere. Some 40 meteorites ranging in size from 0.04 lbs (20 g) to 4 lbs (1.8 kg) were collected.

CHANGING SURFACE ▼

When a meteorite travels through Earth's atmosphere, friction causes its surface to heat up. Inside it stays cool, but its surface melts and much of it is boiled away, leaving behind a bright trail of gas and dust. This stony-iron is one of a number found in Brahin, Belarus, since the early 1800s.

◀ LARGEST METEORITE

The Hoba West is the largest known meteorite. It remains at the spot where it landed in Namibia, where it is a tourist attraction. It was found by chance in 1920 and then weighed 66 tons. Today, it weighs about 6 tons less due to the loss of material that has rusted away. It measures approximately 9.8 ft (3 m) by 9.8 ft (3 m) by 3.3 ft (1 m).

EYE IN THE SKY
The Hubble Space Telescope peers away from Earth and into the universe as it orbits our planet. The first optical telescope to work from orbit, Hubble has been observing space objects since 1990.

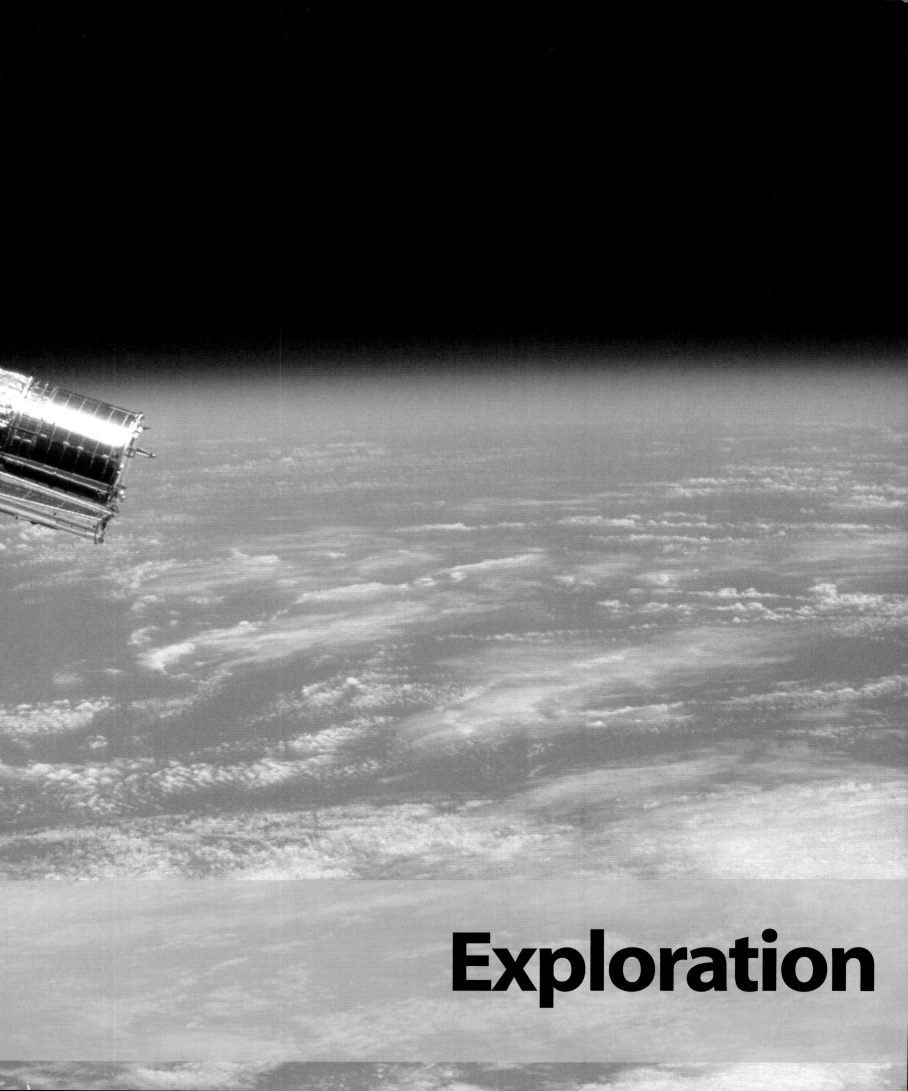

Exploration

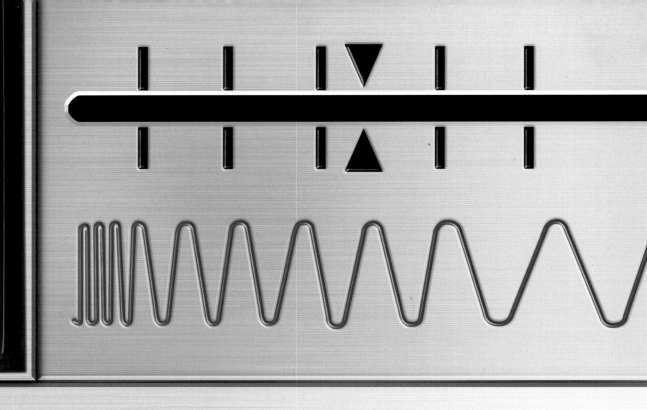

INFORMATION FROM SPACE

One way that astronomers investigate the universe is to study the radiation that its objects emit. This is sent out in all directions and travels at 186,282 miles (299,792 km) per second. Our eyes are sensitive to one form of it—visible light. Light and the other forms of radiation travel in waves and together they make up the electromagnetic spectrum. Astronomers detect the radiation using telescopes, and they get a more complete view of the universe by collecting all types of radiation.

▼ GAMMA RAYS

The brightest gamma and X-ray source in the sky is the Crab Nebula, in the constellation of Taurus. It is the supernova remnant of a star that blew up in 1054. Today, we see the remnant along with its central, super-dense, and extremely hot pulsar, shown here (right) along with another pulsar (top left) at gamma ray wavelengths. The Crab Nebula pulsar spins 30.2 times per second and emits pulses of energy.

▼ X RAYS

X rays and gamma rays are emitted by material that has a temperature of around 1.8 million °F (1 million °C) and by highly energetic electrons as they slow down. The main source in the Crab Nebula is in its central region, which is strongly affected by the pulsar, its stellar wind, and its magnetic field. This X-ray view shows rings of material that have been heated up and thrown out by the star. The activity occupies the inner part of the nebula and is about one light-year across.

▼ ULTRAVIOLET

The ultraviolet emitting region of the Crab Nebula is larger than the region emitting X rays. This radiation is produced by cooler electrons slowing down and losing ultraviolet energy. The central pulsar, which is only about 12.4 miles (20 km) across, energizes these electrons, but they only travel a couple of light years or so before they have lost all their energy and convert back to neutral elements. The movement of the electrons is confined strongly by the pulsar's magnetic field.

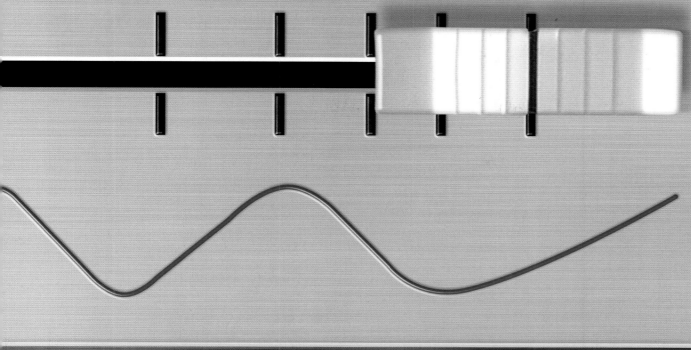

▼ VISIBLE LIGHT

An oval-shaped, 5.5 light-year wide network of filaments emits visible light in the Crab Nebula. These are all that remain of the original star's outer layers that were pushed off in the explosion. They consist of mainly hydrogen and helium, but carbon, oxygen, nitrogen, iron, neon, and sulphur are also present. The filaments contain about 1,300 particles for every cubic centimeter, and have a temperature of up to 32,430 °F (18,000 °C). If visible, the pulsar would be a tiny dot in the centre.

▼ INFRARED

This view of the Crab Nebula combines images taken by the Spitzer Space Telescope at wavelengths of 3.6, 8.0, and 24 microns, all of which fall within the infrared part of the electromagnetic spectrum. Different wavelengths, even when within one type of radiation, often reveal an alternative view. The blue region (3.6 microns) reveals the cloud of electrons trapped within the star's magnetic field. The regions colored yellow-red (8.0 and 24 microns) are the filaments that are we can see in visible light.

▼ RADIO WAVES

The Crab Nebula's radio waves come from electrons which are losing energy as they spiral around the complex of magnetic-field lines surrounding the pulsar. This is the synchrotron process of producing radiation. The electrons are produced by the collisions between the elements in the expanding gas. False colors show the strength of the radio emission. Red is the most intense, yellow less so, then green and blue. The white spot at the center shows the radio pulses the pulsar emits every sixtieth of a second.

▲ ELECTROMAGNETIC SPECTRUM

The radiation in the electromagnetic spectrum travels in waves of differing lengths. Longest are the radio waves, which are usually a meter long. Infrared is in the 1 micron (micron = a millionth of a meter) to 100 micron range. Light varies from violet at around 400 nm (nanometer = a billionth of a meter) to red at 700 nm. Ultraviolet is smaller at around 100 nm, and X rays and gamma rays are shorter still at around 1 nm and 0.01 nm.

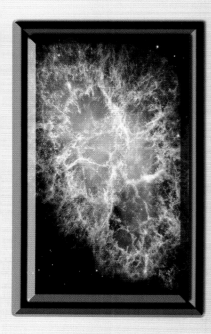

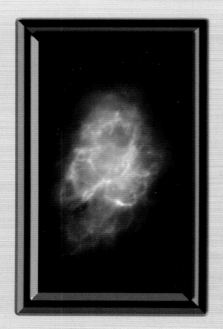

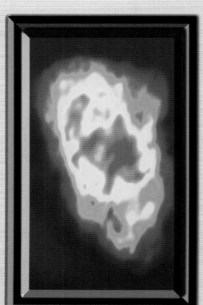

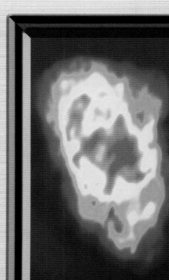

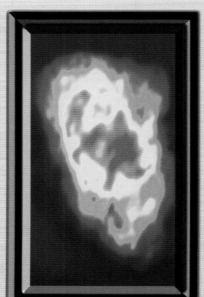

ASTRONOMERS

Astronomers are scientists who study the universe. The first were interested only in how the objects moved. Today, astronomers concentrate on what the objects are like, as well as their origin and evolution. Objects are observed and information collected, and using science and mathematics the astronomer works out more about them. Most of an astronomer's time is spent collating, analyzing, and interpreting the data.

❶ ARTHUR EDDINGTON

In the 1920s, English astronomer Arthur Eddington investigated the interior of stars and realized that they remain stable because of the delicate balance between the pressure exerted by radiation pushing out and the gravitational force pulling in. He also showed that a star's energy comes from nuclear reactions deep inside it.

❷ CECILIA PAYNE-GAPOSCHKIN

As a student, Cecilia Payne was inspired to become an astronomer after attending a lecture by Arthur Eddington. She became the first woman professor of astronomy at Harvard University. In the 1920s, she discovered that stars are made mainly of hydrogen and helium.

❸ FRED HOYLE

Cambridge University astronomer Fred Hoyle is famed for discovering how elements are produced in the centers of stars. Hoyle was also an eminent cosmologist—an astronomer interested in how the universe started, how it developed, and what its future will be. He invented the term "big bang" in 1950, although he didn't believe in it. Hoyle was also a great popularizer of astronomy and an accomplished writer of science fiction.

❹ FRED WHIPPLE

An expert on the minor bodies of the solar system, Fred Whipple was the director of the Smithsonian Astrophysical Observatory at Harvard. In 1949, he suggested that the nucleus of a comet is a dirty snowball—a spinning ball of water snow and rocky dust. He also explained how comets could produce meteor showers and discovered six comets.

❺ SUBRAHMANYAN CHANDRASEKHAR

Nobel Prize–winning astronomer Subrahmanyan Chandrasekhar is most celebrated for his investigation into the way dying stars become either white dwarfs or neutron stars depending on the amount of material they are made of. The Chandra X-ray Observatory space telescope is named after him.

❻ EDWIN HUBBLE

Discoveries made by Edwin Hubble in the 1920s changed our ideas on the universe. While using the Hooker telescope at Mount Wilson Observatory, California, Hubble discovered that the universe contains galaxies beyond the Milky Way. His studies of the structure of galaxies led him to classify them according to shape. In 1929, Hubble realized that galaxies are moving away and the universe is expanding. The Hubble Space Telescope is named after him.

❼ EUGENE SHOEMAKER

When a health problem prevented geologist Eugene Shoemaker from traveling to the Moon, he did the next best thing. He trained the Apollo astronauts in geological techniques to be used on the Moon's surface. Later, he searched the sky for asteroids, discovering Comet Shoemaker-Levy 9 in 1993. After his death, his ashes made it to the Moon aboard the Lunar Prospector spacecraft.

❾ RICCARDO GIACCONI

Awarded the Nobel Prize for Physics in 2002, Riccardo Giacconi has been the director of both the Space Telescope Science Institute, which controls the use of the Hubble Space Telescope, and of the European Southern Observatory. He has devised these instruments for detecting X rays emitted by stars and fitted these instruments to a range of spacecraft, including the Chandra X-ray Observatory.

❿ JAN OORT

Most of this Dutch astronomer's working life was spent as the director of the Leiden Observatory, in the Netherlands. In 1927, when he was still a young man, he confirmed that the Milky Way Galaxy rotates. In the 1940s, Oort was one of the first to realize the potential of radio astronomy. His name lives on in the Oort Cloud, the huge cloud of comets that he suggested surrounds the solar system.

❽ VERA RUBIN

Working at the Carnegie Institute, Washington, Vera Rubin studied galaxies. She was particularly interested in the orbital motion of stars around the centers of galaxies. She found that the stars move as if the galaxy contains many times more material than that in its stars. In 1983, Rubin concluded that about 90 percent of the material in the galaxies she had been studying was in the form of dark matter.

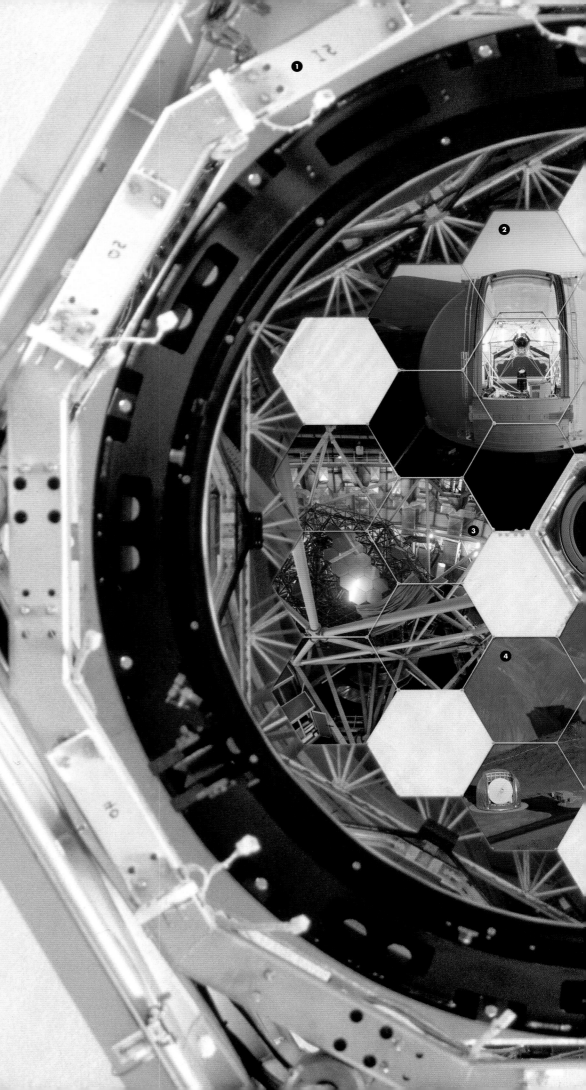

TELESCOPES

Astronomers have been using telescopes to explore the Universe for 400 years. Telescopes magnify distant objects and let astronomers see them more clearly. The first collected only visible light, but since the middle of the 1900s, telescopes have collected a range of wavelengths. Those based on Earth collect optical, radio, and infrared waves. They collect the wavelengths and then focus them to form an image of the object under study.

❶ MAIN MIRROR

A key part of an optical telescope is its main mirror. This collects the light, and the bigger the mirror is, the more the astronomer sees. The 33-ft (10-m) wide mirror of the Keck II telescope is constructed from 36 hexagonal segments. If made in one piece, the mirror would have sagged under its own weight. Each of the segments is computer controlled and adjusted twice a second to counteract distortions due to gravity.

❷ KECK II

The main mirror of the Keck II telescope is visible below the telescope's open metal structure. Keck II and its neighbor Keck I are two of the world's largest optical telescopes. They are located on Mauna Kea in Hawaii and work independently or together. Both use adaptive optics, a system that compensates for atmospheric blurring and sharpens the image.

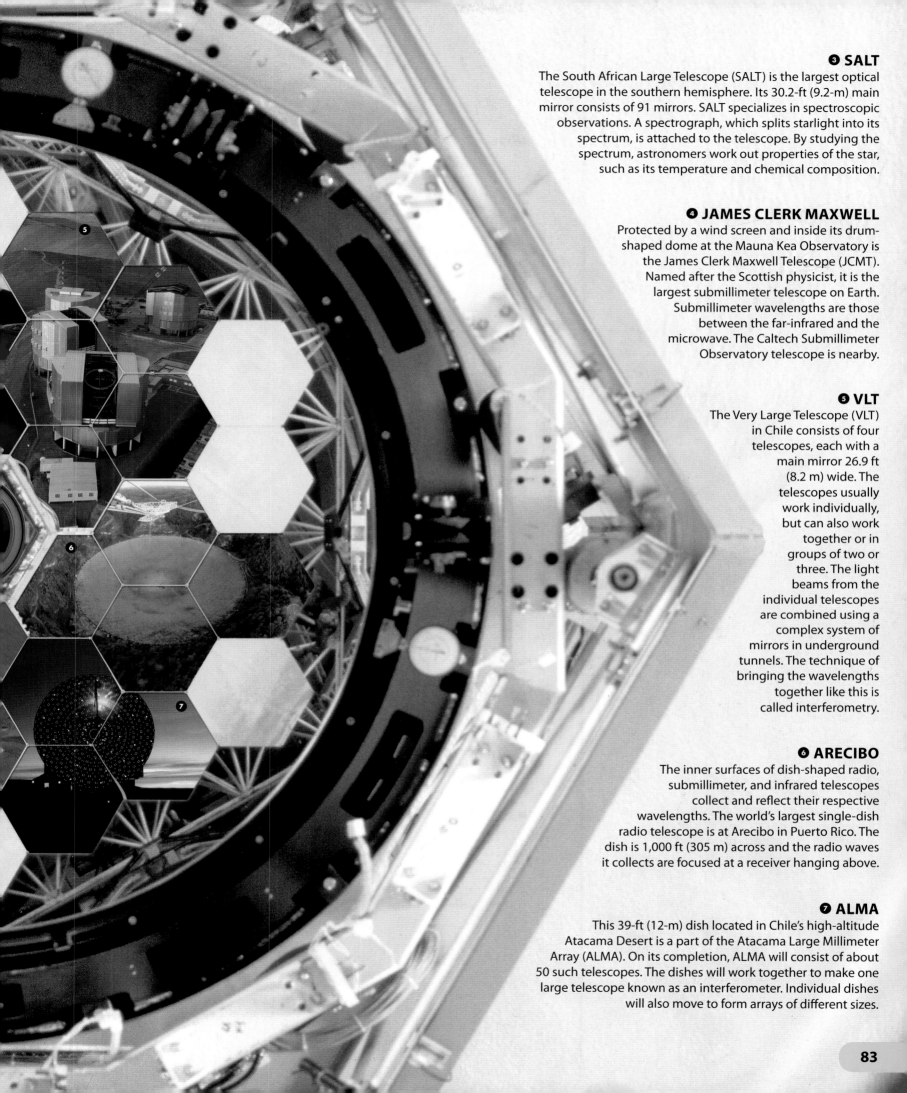

❸ SALT

The South African Large Telescope (SALT) is the largest optical telescope in the southern hemisphere. Its 30.2-ft (9.2-m) main mirror consists of 91 mirrors. SALT specializes in spectroscopic observations. A spectrograph, which splits starlight into its spectrum, is attached to the telescope. By studying the spectrum, astronomers work out properties of the star, such as its temperature and chemical composition.

❹ JAMES CLERK MAXWELL

Protected by a wind screen and inside its drum-shaped dome at the Mauna Kea Observatory is the James Clerk Maxwell Telescope (JCMT). Named after the Scottish physicist, it is the largest submillimeter telescope on Earth. Submillimeter wavelengths are those between the far-infrared and the microwave. The Caltech Submillimeter Observatory telescope is nearby.

❺ VLT

The Very Large Telescope (VLT) in Chile consists of four telescopes, each with a main mirror 26.9 ft (8.2 m) wide. The telescopes usually work individually, but can also work together or in groups of two or three. The light beams from the individual telescopes are combined using a complex system of mirrors in underground tunnels. The technique of bringing the wavelengths together like this is called interferometry.

❻ ARECIBO

The inner surfaces of dish-shaped radio, submillimeter, and infrared telescopes collect and reflect their respective wavelengths. The world's largest single-dish radio telescope is at Arecibo in Puerto Rico. The dish is 1,000 ft (305 m) across and the radio waves it collects are focused at a receiver hanging above.

❼ ALMA

This 39-ft (12-m) dish located in Chile's high-altitude Atacama Desert is a part of the Atacama Large Millimeter Array (ALMA). On its completion, ALMA will consist of about 50 such telescopes. The dishes will work together to make one large telescope known as an interferometer. Individual dishes will also move to form arrays of different sizes.

OBSERVATORY

The majority of the world's most powerful telescopes are sited at mountain-top locations around our planet. Often many telescopes occupy the same site, each usually protected inside its own building. Together with the workshops, offices, canteens, and sleeping quarters for the astronomers, they make up an observatory. At their high-altitude sites, the air is clear, still, dry, and thin, and the observatories are away from city lights. From here, astronomers look up into the clearest, darkest skies and get the best possible views of the universe.

❶ KITT PEAK

Located high in the Quinlan Mountains in Arizona, the Kitt Peak National Observatory houses 26 optical telescopes and two radio telescopes. This makes the observatory the largest collection of astronomical instruments in the world. Almost three-quarters of the nights here are clear, and in the daytime, the McMath-Pierce Solar Telescope, the largest optical solar telescope in the world, takes advantage of the clear sky.

❷ CALAR ALTO

Observatories are expensive, so national governments and universities often cooperate to share the costs. The German and Spanish governments came together to fund and build the Calar Alto Observatory in the 1970s. It is situated at a height of 7,113 ft (2,168 m), near the peak of Mount Calar Alto in southern Spain. From here, the observatory's five large telescopes can observe all the northern hemisphere sky and part of the southern sky.

The dome of the Mayall telescope stands behind the Bok telescope dome; both are optical telescopes

❶

Inside the dome is a 7.2-ft (2.2-m) telescope

❷

Four identical buildings each house a VLT telescope

❸

❸ EUROPEAN SOUTHERN OBSERVATORY

The European Southern Observatory (ESO) is run by 14 European countries on three separate sites in the Atacama Desert, Chile. Its main site is at Paranal, at an altitude of 8,645 ft (2,635 m) in the Andes Mountains. The largest telescope here is the Very Large Telescope (VLT), which is made up of four separate 26.9-ft (8.2-m) telescopes. Facilities include accommodation, restaurants, and gardens.

❹ MAUNA KEA

In the middle of the Pacific Ocean and on the summit of the Mauna Kea volcano on the Big Island of Hawaii, is one of the best observing locations in the world. At 13,205 ft (4,205 m) high, this site is above the majority of the water vapour in Earth's atmosphere. It is a multinational site and several countries have telescopes or a part-share in a telescope here. The Keck telescopes are run by a research group based in California, while the Subaru telescope is owned and run by Japan.

❺ PARKES RADIO DISH

Telescopes that collect shortwave radio waves are located at mountain-top sites. However, other radio waves are unaffected by Earth's atmosphere, so the telescopes that collect them can be located at low altitude. The 210-ft (64-m) radio telescope dish of the Parkes Observatory in Australia is computer-controlled and continually changes its orientation in order to track a source as it moves across the sky.

Keck telescope dome

Parkes is the second biggest steerable radio dish in the southern hemisphere

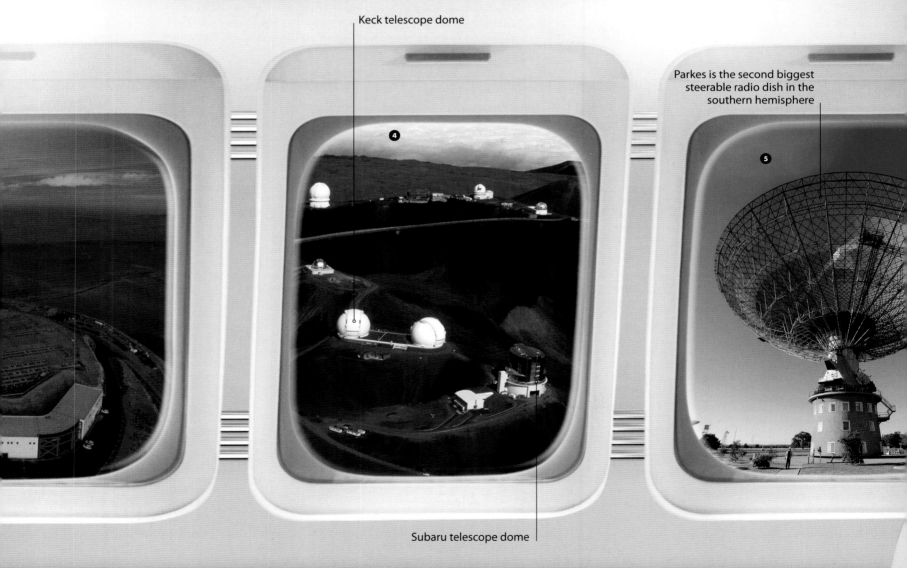

Subaru telescope dome

ROCKETS

Anything or anyone that leaves Earth to travel into space needs a rocket. The rocket's power lifts it and its cargo off the ground and away from the pull of Earth's gravity. Gas produced by the rocket's fuel is forced out of the bottom of the rocket at high speed, and this propels the rocket upward. Rockets have been lifting off and heading for space for more than 60 years. They are launched from one of about 30 launch sites around the world. Most sites are located close to Earth's equator, so that the rockets benefit from Earth's spin speed as they take off.

▼ ROCKET SCIENCE

Most space rockets use two liquid fuels that are combined in the combustion chamber found at the base of all rockets. Once ignited, the fuels form very hot, high-pressure gas, which is ejected through the rocket's base nozzle. The downward momentum of the gas pushes the rocket upwards. The more fuel burned, the lighter the rocket becomes and the faster it goes. It needs a speed of 7 miles (11.3 km) per second to escape Earth's gravity.

▶ PAYLOAD

A rocket's cargo is known as its payload and is usually a satellite, or a manned or unmanned spacecraft. The weight of the rocket and its fuel is typically 20 to 100 times greater than the weight of the payload being launched. Within the nose part of this Soyuz FG rocket is the TMA-13 spacecraft with its three astronauts. They are leaving the Baikonur Cosmodrome in Kazakhstan for the International Space Station. The access gantries to left and right pull back just before ignition.

▶ ROCKET STAGES

The simplest rockets consist of one stage, which is ignited on the launch pad. Many rockets use two or three stages, each of which contain their own engines and propellant fuels. When the first stage, which is the lowest, runs out of fuel, it is jettisoned and the stage above it is ignited. The remaining rocket is now lighter, enabling its second and third stages to lift a payload into orbit. This image shows a Saturn V second stage above Earth.

▼ ION DRIVE

Traditional rockets provide a high thrust for a short time. The ion drive system provides a low thrust for a long time, but very high speeds are ultimately achieved. The thrust is generated by ionized atoms of the gas xenon being pushed out of the back of the engine. Although this system lacks the huge thrust needed for a launch, it can propel spacecraft through space.

Ion engine being tested—faint blue glow is ionized atoms emitted from engine

▶ LAUNCHPAD

The immediate area and facilities from which a rocket lifts off is called the launch pad. A launch site usually has a number of pads. Associated with are built up the side of the pad is a which are built. At the base of the pad is a service equipment structure the engines. During the flame deflection by the rocket is stabilized the heat generated the rocket powers up to full thrust. first seconds after ignition the rocket powers up to full thrust.

A Proton-M rocket is ready to launch from the Baikonur Cosmodrome, in Kazakhstan

SATELLITES

Hundreds of artificial satellites are orbiting Earth at any one time. The orbits they follow depend on the work they do. Craft that need to stay over a particular place on Earth's surface are in geostationary orbit. They orbit 22,227 miles (35,786 km) above the equator, keeping pace with Earth's spin. Many others are in low Earth orbit. At a height of only a few hundred miles, they circle every 1.5 hours and cover the whole planet. Others follow a path that takes them over Earth's poles.

EARTH OBSERVING ▶

Satellites that monitor the natural state of our planet are known as Earth observing satellites. They collect information on its land, water, ice, and atmosphere, recording short- and long-term changes. In this way, they monitor processes such as agriculture, deforestation, and ground water movement. Building activities, forest fires, floods, and pollution are also mapped. Some countries use satellites to spy on other nations.

▼ WEATHER WATCHERS

A global weather watch is provided by satellites from the U.S., Europe, India, China, Japan, and Russia. Their cameras and radiation equipment monitor cloud systems, snow and ice cover, and ocean currents. Those in geostationary orbit constantly monitor one region. Others pass over Earth's poles and these observe any place on Earth twice a day.

CloudSat provides information on Earth's clouds, snow, and rain

Europe's Envisat, launched in 2002, is the largest Earth-observing satellite

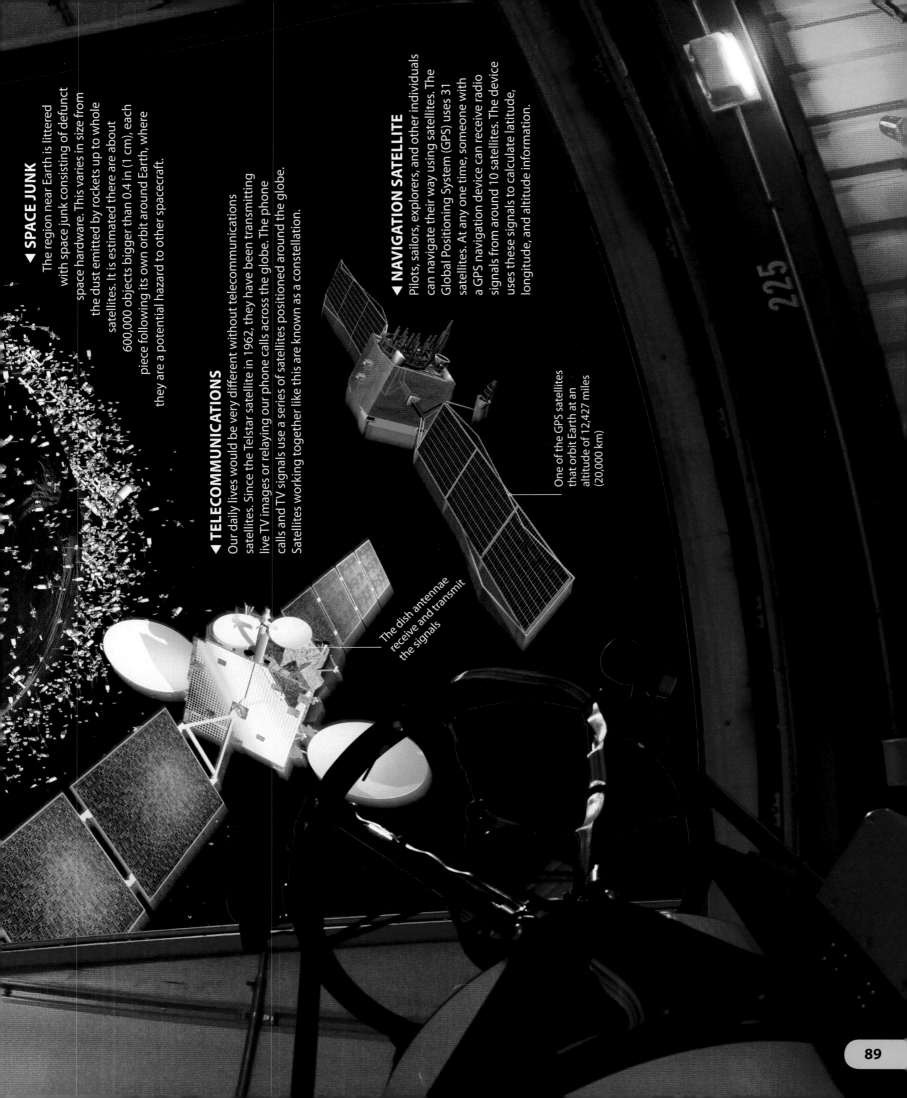

▼ SPACE JUNK

The region near Earth is littered with space junk consisting of defunct space hardware. This varies in size from the dust emitted by rockets up to whole satellites. It is estimated there are about 600,000 objects bigger than 0.4 in (1 cm), each piece following its own orbit around Earth, where they are a potential hazard to other spacecraft.

▼ TELECOMMUNICATIONS

Our daily lives would be very different without telecommunications satellites. Since the Telstar satellite in 1962, they have been transmitting live TV images or relaying our phone calls across the globe. The phone calls and TV signals use a series of satellites positioned around the globe. Satellites working together like this are known as a constellation.

The dish antennae receive and transmit the signals

▼ NAVIGATION SATELLITE

Pilots, sailors, explorers, and other individuals can navigate their way using satellites. The Global Positioning System (GPS) uses 31 satellites. At any one time, someone with a GPS navigation device can receive radio signals from around 10 satellites. The device uses these signals to calculate latitude, longitude, and altitude information.

One of the GPS satellites that orbit Earth at an altitude of 12,427 miles (20,000 km)

SPACE TELESCOPES

Astronomers have been using space-based telescopes for about 40 years. Some of these telescopes orbit our planet, while others orbit the Sun, while near Earth. Space telescopes are usually designed to work in one specific wavelength band, such as X ray or infrared. They collect and record data in much the same way that telescopes do on Earth, but space telescopes work all year round, day and night, and they are built to last for several years without repair.

Solar panels provide power which is stored in three banks of batteries

CHANDRA ▶

Launched in 1999, the Chandra X-ray Observatory studies the more energetic regions of the Universe. It moves along an elliptical orbit around Earth, looking at, among other things, the remnants of exploded stars and the regions around black holes. X rays are collected and focused by four mirrors nested inside each other. The information is recorded by instruments at the end of the telescope's 45-ft (13.7-m) body.

A sunshade protects the telescope from the Sun's heat

Secondary mirror reflects radiation to instruments

◀ HERSCHEL

The 11.5-feet (3.5-m) wide mirror of the Herschel Space Observatory is the largest single mirror of any space telescope. It collects infrared wavelengths from dusty and cold objects. The telescope stays cool to make sure its own heat doesn't spoil its observations. Liquid helium keeps its temperature down to almost -459°F (-273°C). The telescope is expected to work for at least three years.

Main mirror reflects wavelengths to secondary mirror

Tank contains liquid helium to cool the instruments

FIRST VIEW ▶

This is the first picture taken by Herschel in June 2009—an image of the Whirlpool Galaxy. The blue regions are warm dust heated by young stars. Colder dust appears red-brown. The brightest blue dot at the top is a smaller companion galaxy.

The sunshade shields the entrance to the telescope from the Sun

Mirror assembly

Thrusters used after launch to propel Chandra to its orbit

FIRST DECADE ▶

This Chandra image of the center of the Milky Way Galaxy was produced in late 2009 to mark 10 successful years of observations. It is a combination of 88 observations taken over a period of a little over 26 days. It shows the region around the supermassive black hole Sagittarius A* in the center of the galaxy. The black hole is within the bright area at the center of the image.

Aperture door is closed during servicing missions to protect the mirrors

ORION NEBULA ▶

All four of Hubble's cameras and imaging instruments were used to produce this view of the Orion Nebula. The data for it was collected as Hubble made 105 orbits of Earth. Among the 3,000 stars that Hubble revealed in this region are what seem to be young brown dwarfs. These are failed stars: They are made of too little material to get hot enough to shine.

HUBBLE ▲

The Hubble Space Telescope works about 348 miles (560 km) above Earth as it orbits the planet. Its 8-ft (2.4-m) main mirror started collecting infrared, visible, and ultraviolet radiation from distant objects in 1990. Once recorded by its cameras and other instruments, the data is passed to satellites in the Tracking and Data Relay Satellite System. It is then forwarded to receiving stations on Earth.

WORKING LIFE ▶

Space telescopes are usually built to last several years without repair, but the Hubble Space Telescope is the exception. Astronauts visited Hubble five times between 1993 and 2009, servicing the telescope, making repairs, and replacing parts. Here, Jeff Hoffman removes the original Wide Field and Planetary Camera before replacing it in 1993.

ROBOTIC EXPLORERS

Unmanned robotic spacecraft have been exploring nearby space for about 50 years. About 200 of them have been launched from Earth, but only about half have been successful. These robotic explorers have visited all the planets, Earth's Moon, other planetary moons, asteroids, and comets, and approached the Sun. Most craft have been sent by the U.S. and Russia, but in recent years Europe, Japan, China, and India have sent them too.

Cassini has measured the sizes of particles that make up Saturn's rings

NEW HORIZONS ▶

In January 2006, New Horizons started its journey to Pluto. It is carrying investigative tools such as cameras and a dust detector, as well as a computer, which is the craft's brain, communications equipment, and a power source. New Horizons is a flyby craft—it will arrive at Pluto in 2015 and make observations as it flies past the dwarf planet en route for the Kuiper Belt.

Information sent to Earth through the dish antenna

ROSETTA ▶

Robotic craft travel to places too dangerous or remote for humans, and they perform monotonous jobs over long periods of time. After a journey lasting 10 years, Rosetta will arrive at the Comet Churyumov-Gerasimenko in 2014. The craft will stay with the comet nucleus for eight years as it travels in towards the Sun, around it, and then away again. Rosetta will release a smaller craft, called Philae, to land on the comet's surface.

▼ CASSINI-HUYGENS

Spacecraft sent to explore the planets and their moons are typically the size of a car or a small bus. The Cassini-Huygens craft is one of the largest ever built—it is about 23 ft (7 m) long and 13 ft (4 m) wide. As its name suggests, it consists of two parts. In 2004, the main craft, Cassini, moved into orbit around Saturn, and has been investigating the planet and its moons ever since. The smaller craft, Huygens, was released by Cassini and parachuted to the surface of Saturn's largest moon, Titan, sending back pictures of the moon's surface.

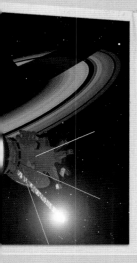

▼ NEAR

Unlike astronauts, spacecraft don't need to return home once their work is done. NEAR, the first craft to land on an asteroid, is still there. Initially designed to just orbit the asteroid Eros for one year, the mission ended with a touchdown on February 12, 2001.

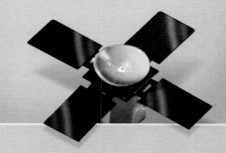

▼ MARS EXPRESS

Some robotic craft investigate a planet as they fly past, whereas others do so as they orbit it. Mars Express moved into a polar orbit around the planet Mars in January 2004. As it travelled to within 300 km (186 miles) of the Martian surface, its seven instruments started to record data. It was initially going to monitor the planet for one Martian year (687 Earth days), but Mars Express proved so successful that its life has been extended twice.

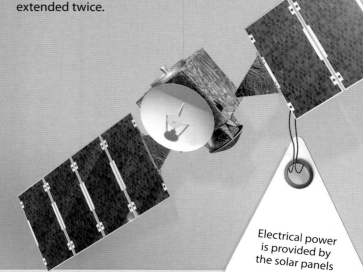

Electrical power is provided by the solar panels

◄ VOYAGER

The twin craft Voyager 1 and Voyager 2 made a grand tour of the giant planets between 1979 and 1989. They both flew by Jupiter and Saturn, and Voyager 2 went on to fly by Uranus and Neptune. Voyager 2 remains the only craft to visit these two planets. Voyager 1 is now more than 10.4 billion miles (16.8 billion km) away, the most distant spacecraft from Earth, and more than 100 times farther from the Sun than Earth. It is getting more distant by about 10.6 miles (17 km) every second and is still communicating with Earth.

▼ STARDUST

A very few space missions have returned to Earth with a sample of a space object. The first were the three Russian Luna craft that returned with soil from the Moon in the 1970s. Stardust collected dust from Comet Wild 2 while flying through its coma in 2004. It returned the sample to Earth in a capsule in January 2006. Meanwhile, Stardust has a new target—it will fly past Comet Tempel 1 in February 2011.

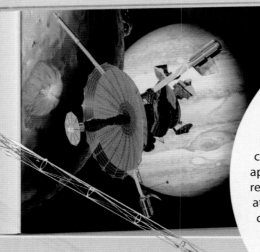

◄ GALILEO

The Galileo craft spent eight years studying Jupiter and its moons between 1995 and 2003. It orbited the planet roughly every two months, following long paths that brought it close to all the major moons. When it initially approached the planet, Galileo released a probe into Jupiter's atmosphere. Once the main craft ceased working, it was deliberately crashed into Jupiter.

ROVERS ON MARS

Five of the robotic craft sent out from Earth to explore the solar system have been rovers. These craft are designed to drive across alien terrain, stopping now and again to make on-the-spot investigations. The first two, Lunokhod 1 and Lunokhod 2, explored the Moon in the early 1970s. The other three were sent to Mars, and two are still working there now. The rovers' solar panels power both the craft and their suite of instruments, including cameras and rock analysis tools.

❶ SOJOURNER

The first rover to Mars was a microwave-oven sized buggy called *Sojourner*. It was carried to the planet by the landing craft Mars Pathfinder, arriving there on July 4, 1997. The landing site was a rock-strewn, ancient floodplain called Ares Vallis. *Sojourner* worked for almost three months, analyzing the chemical properties of rocks. *Sojourner* returned some 550 photographs back to Earth.

❷ SPIRIT

Two identical craft arrived on Mars in 2004. The first was *Spirit*, which touched down on January 4 at Gusev Crater. It drove over about 5 miles (8 km) of the crater's floor, before it became stuck in loose soil in May 2009. *Spirit* has found basaltic rock, which is evidence that volcanic lava once flowed here, and older sedimentary rock, which indicates the presence of water in the past.

Pancam consists of two digital cameras which can turn 360° and take panoramic views

X-ray spectrometer tested composition of rock and soil samples

❸ OPPORTUNITY

Opportunity is working on the opposite side of Mars to *Spirit*. It arrived at Meridiani Planum on January 25, 2004, and has traversed 11.7 miles (18 km) of the Martian surface, stopping to investigate the three impact craters Endurance, Erebus, and Victoria. *Opportunity* and *Spirit* have a jointed arm that extends out at the front of the lower body. The arm's array of instruments examines rock and soil. Collected data is relayed to Earth via Mars Odyssey and Mars Global Surveyor, which are orbiting Mars.

❹ LANDING CASING

Spirit and *Opportunity* travelled to Mars inside identical landing craft. A parachute slowed each lander's descent to the surface and four airbags cushioned the craft's touchdown. Once the lander had come to a halt, the airbags were deflated and pulled towards the lander to leave the surrounding area clear for the rover. The sides of the lander opened like flower petals, making the rover upright in the process, in readiness to drive out of the lander.

❺ ROCKY TERRAIN

Rovers sent to Mars are designed and tested to cope with its surface terrain. *Spirit* and *Opportunity* were built to roll along at about 2 in (5 cm) per second, stopping several times a minute to study the ground around them. They avoided surface holes, large rocks, steep slopes, and sand traps. A suspension system kept their wheels on the ground when crossing rough surfaces, and their wheels were designed to provide grip on the rocky soil.

The deflated airbags and lander casing that brought *Opportunity* to Mars

Low-gain antenna, one of three antennae used for communications

SEARCH FOR LIFE

Our home planet, Earth, is the only place in the universe where we know for certain that life exists. Life may occur elsewhere—it would be extraordinary if it didn't, as the chemical elements found in all Earth's living things are found throughout the universe. In recent decades, we have started looking for extraterrestrial life. It could be in one of a number of forms, from microorganisms to primitive creatures, and even complex and intelligent beings. Our search started in the solar system, but now includes planets around distant stars.

LIFE ON EARTH ▶

Life on Earth began about 3.8 billion years ago when carbon-containing molecules in Earth's oceans evolved into tiny cells. Life now consists of at least 1.5 million different types, or species—from single-cell forms, such as bacteria, to multicellular animals, including humans. Most scientists think that extraterrestrial life will be similar to Earth's.

SENDING MESSAGES ▶

Spacecraft sent out from Earth to explore the solar system have carried plaques and disks containing information about humans and the planet we live on. Voyager 1 and Voyager 2 left Earth in 1977. On board each was a gold-plated disk with sounds and images of life on our planet. Voyager 1 is now the farthest artificial body from Earth, but it will be 40,000 years before it approaches another planetary system.

LISTENING FOR SIGNS ▲

The Allen Telescope Array, California, has been listening for signals from extraterrestrial life since 2007. It consists of 42 radio dishes that are directed towards nearby Sunlike stars. More dishes will be added, until a total of 350 will work together. They are part of a search called SETI (Search for Extraterrestrial Intelligence). No messages sent deliberately or by chance have been received, so far.

▲ PLANET HUNTING

Earthlike planets orbiting distant stars are good places to search for life. In 2009, the Kepler spacecraft started a search for such planets by monitoring 100,000 stars. A planet is detected when it causes a dip in brightness as it crosses in front of the star it orbits.

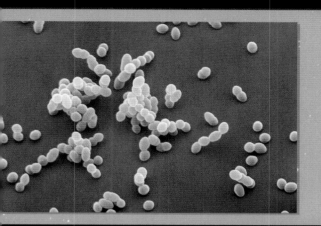

FICTIONAL ALIENS ▶

Authors and artists have imagined strange creatures living on other solar system worlds for more than 200 years. From the 1930s to 1950s, alien invasions of Earth featured regularly in comics, books, and films. In October 1938, people in the U.S. were temporarily convinced that Martians had landed when they mistook a radio version of H G Wells' novel *The War of the Worlds* as a news bulletin.

◀ LOOKING ON MARS ▶

Mars is the only solar system planet, apart from Earth, that astronomers believe could be home to life. Any life that may have developed there would be microbial and formed when the planet was young. Two Viking spacecraft landed on Mars in 1976 and tested the planet's soils for signs of life, but the results were inconclusive. The rover *Curiosity* will travel there in 2011 and assess whether Mars can or ever could have supported microbial life.

EARTHLIKE EXOPLANET ▶

Once Earthlike planets are found, the next stage is to assess how many are in the habitable zone—the region around a star where the temperature is right for liquid water and where life could develop. Analysis of the planets' atmospheres would also reveal any chemical compounds we associate with life. This could be oxygen that has come from plants, or methane and carbon dioxide given out by animals.

FUTURE EXPLORERS

As one generation of spacecraft investigates the universe, future missions are being planned and built. The design and manufacture of a craft can take years, and, in the process, it undergoes rigorous tests. Even after launch, it can be months or years before a craft reaches its target and sets to work. Future robotic craft will return to worlds already visited to explore them in greater detail, while others investigate new targets. Closer to home, new space telescopes will peer into deep space as well as observe and monitor nearby worlds.

▼ JUNO

In 2011, the Juno spacecraft will start its journey to Jupiter. After arrival in 2016, it will spend the next 12 months travelling round the planet from pole to pole. Juno spins around three times per minute as it travels. As a result, Juno's instruments, which are placed around its body, will observe Jupiter about 400 times in the two hours the craft takes to fly from pole to pole. The information collected will help us to learn about Jupiter's atmosphere, what lies beneath it, and the planet's origins.

▲ GRAIL

The Gravity Recovery and Interior Laboratory (GRAIL) mission consists of twin spacecraft. The pair will launch together in 2011, and fly around the Moon over a three-month period. Measurements of data transmitted between themselves and Earth along with knowledge of the relative positions of the craft will be used to measure the Moon's gravity. The results will give an insight into what lies beneath the Moon's surface and what its internal structure is like from crust to core.

▲ CURIOSITY

A rover called Curiosity and officially known as the Mars Science Laboratory mission will head off to Mars in late 2011. About the size of a small car, Curiosity will be the largest rover to explore the planet. It also has the capability of travelling farther than any other. It will move over the surface at speeds of up to 295 ft (90 m) per hour, rolling over obstacles up to 29 in (75 cm) high. Soil and rocks will be analyzed by 10 instruments to ascertain whether Mars could support microbial life now, or could have done so in the past.

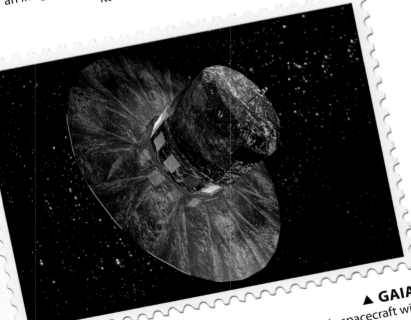

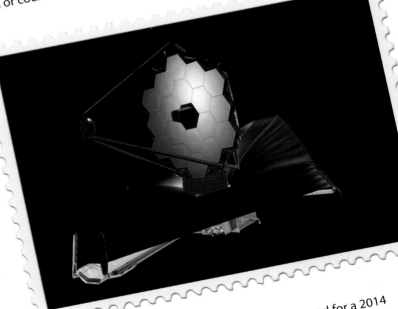

▲ GAIA

Over a five-year period, starting in 2011, the Gaia spacecraft will look at about one million stars in the Milky Way. This space telescope will examine them 100 times each, recording their brightness and position over time. The data, even once compressed, will fill more than 30,000 CDs. It will be used to construct the largest 3-D map of the Milky Way ever produced, and will reveal details of the composition, formation, and evolution of our galaxy.

▲ JAMES WEBB

The James Webb Space Telescope is being prepared for a 2014 launch. Although hailed as the successor to the Hubble Space Telescope, it is different in a number of ways. It works in the infrared and is much larger—its 21.3-ft (6.5-m) main mirror is made from 18 segments. The telescope will be pointed so that the Sun, Earth, and Moon are on one side, and its tennis-court sized sunshield will protect the telescope like a parasol.

LONELY TRAVELER
Astronaut Harrison Schmitt stands next to his lunar rover as he looks into Shorty Crater on the Moon. He is one of 12 people to have walked on the Moon, the only world beyond Earth that humans have visited.

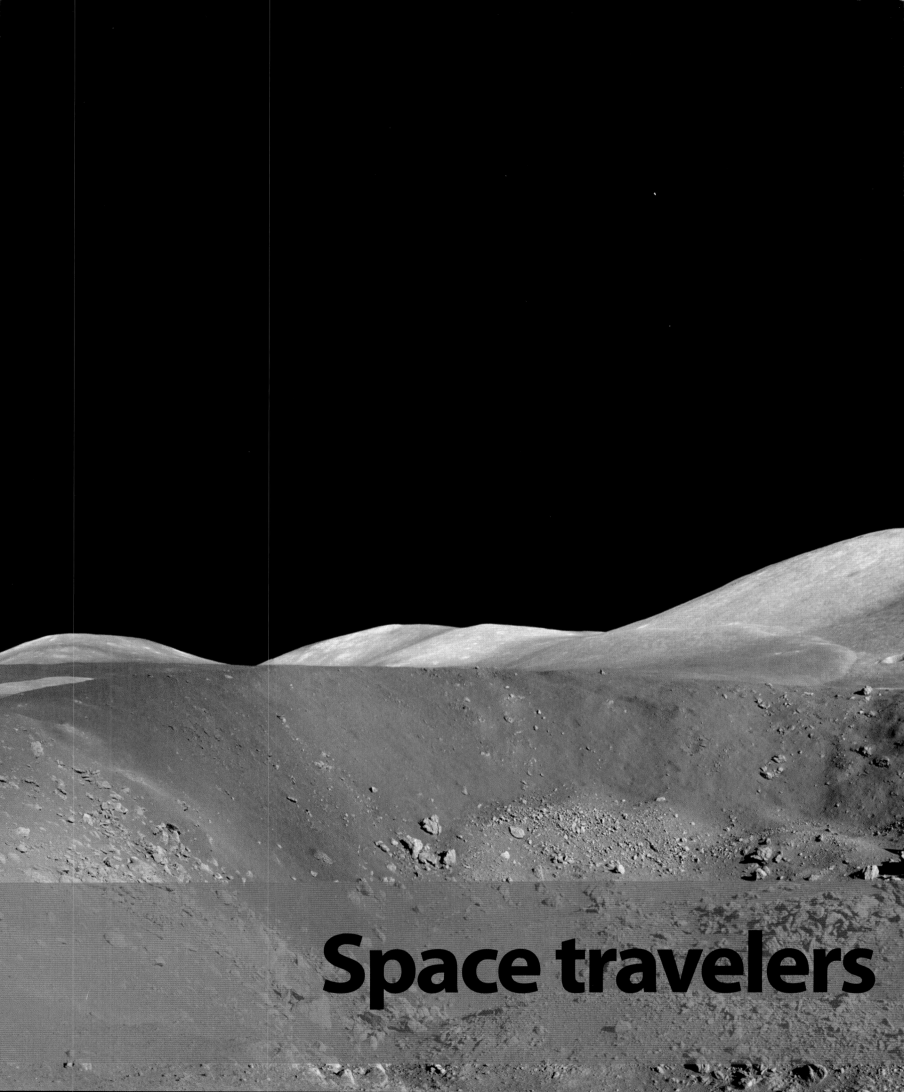

Space travelers

ASTRONAUTS

More than 500 astronauts have traveled into space so far. They have come from about 40 different nations and are mostly men, but the total includes more than 50 women. When the first flew in 1961, just two nations launched astronauts—the Soviet Union and the U.S. In 2003, however, China became the third nation to launch its own astronauts. All of these astronauts, except the 24 who went to the Moon, have traveled only as far as near-Earth space.

❶ FIRST INTO SPACE

The first person into space was the Russian Yuri Gagarin. He traveled once around Earth in Vostok 1 on April 12, 1961, on a journey lasting 108 minutes. He ejected from his craft after it had reentered Earth's atmosphere and parachuted back to the surface. The first woman into space was also Russian, Valentina Tereshkova, who flew into orbit on June 16, 1963.

❷ THE RIGHT STUFF

Potential astronauts applying for selection and training need specific qualities. The U.S. and European agencies look for English-speaking men and women who are aged 27 to 37, and between 60 to 75 in (153 and 190 cm) tall. They need a university degree or an equivalent qualification in a science-based subject.

❸ FIRST AMERICAN

On May 5, 1961, American Alan Shepard became the first American into space. Inside his Shepard achieved the first American and the second man into space, Freedom 7, Shepard capsule, Freedom 7 (187 km), but Shepard an altitude of 116 miles did not orbit the Earth. Shepard later became the fifth man to walk became the commander of the on the Moon as Apollo 14 mission.

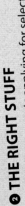

❹ RECORD BREAKER

Sergei Krikalev has spent more time in space than anyone else. He traveled there six times, between November 1988 and October 2005, and stayed for a total of 803.4 days. The record for the longest single stay in space is held by fellow Russian Valeri Poliakov—437.7 days from launch to return to Earth. He made his record stay on the Mir space station between January 1994 and March 1995.

⑤ COMMERCIAL ASTRONAUT

On June 21, 2004, Mike Melvill became the first commercial astronaut when he piloted the privately owned spacecraft SpaceShipOne. He gained his astronaut status by flying to an altitude of more than 62 miles (100 km) above Earth. Prior to his flight, all astronauts had travelled aboard an American, Russian, or Chinese spacecraft that was owned and paid for by the state.

⑥ OLDEST ASTRONAUT

John Glenn has flown into space twice. The first time was in 1962, when he became the first American to orbit Earth inside Friendship 7. He flew again on October 29, 1998 on the space shuttle Discovery for a nine-day mission. By then he was 77 and the oldest astronaut to fly, a record he still holds. The youngest was 25-year-old Russian astronaut Gherman Titov in August 1961.

⑦ MISSION SPECIALIST

Astronauts train for about two years before a mission. This includes classroom study as well as working with space equipment. Once chosen for a flight, astronauts are trained for a particular role, such as pilot or mission commander. In August 2007, Rick Mastracchio was a mission specialist on a shuttle flight to the International Space Station—he was the ascent flight engineer and performed three spacewalks.

⑧ TAIKONAUT

Everyone traveling into space is described as an astronaut (a word that comes from the Greek for "star" and "sailor"). The word cosmonaut is used for someone traveling as part of the Russian space programme, and a taikonaut is a Chinese space traveler. The first Chinese astronaut was Yang Liwei, and his flight, on October 15, 2003, made China the third country capable of launching astronauts.

WEIGHTLESSNESS

Humans live on Earth and we feel the pull of its gravity. This gives us weight. Gravity exists throughout the universe and astronauts encounter it wherever they travel. Those on the Moon felt the pull of its gravity, which is one-sixth the pull of Earth's. Astronauts above Earth are orbiting the planet and feel weightless. They are in free fall: Gravity is pulling them to Earth, but they are moving horizontally around Earth at the same time.

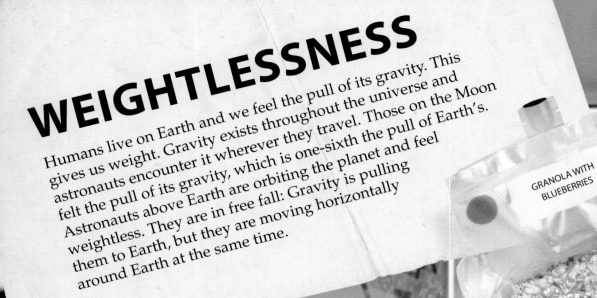

TEA WITH LEMON

LEMON-LIME DRINK

GRANOLA WITH BLUEBERRIES

Food is eaten directly from pouches to prevent spillage

◀ SPACE SENSATION

There is no up or down in an orbiting spacecraft and astronauts move by pushing or pulling themselves using hand holds or anything within reach. Humans adapt to the conditions, but plants cannot orientate themselves: Some send their roots out of the soil and their shoots into it. Spiders are initially confused, but soon learn how to build a web in weightlessness.

Astronaut checks a plant experiment on board the International Space Station

▶ DAILY LIFE

Everyday activities such as drinking, washing, and sleeping need care in a weightless environment. Liquids would float about and so drinks are taken straight from pouches, and astronauts keep clean by using wipes. Sleeping astronauts are tied down to stop them drifting away. Fans circulate the air inside the craft so that astronauts don't breathe in the carbon dioxide they have just breathed out.

Astronaut fixes her feet on the wall to stop herself moving as she uses the laptop

Arms and hair of sleeping astronaut float freely

◄ TRAINING

Astronauts prepare for weightlessness in two ways. They make repeated flights in a specially modified plane that follows a path known as a parabolic loop. As they fly on the downward part of the path, anyone inside feels weightless. Secondly, they train for spacewalks in a huge water tank known as the Neutral Buoyancy Laboratory. Wearing a modified spacesuit, astronauts work with mock-ups of their craft. The underwater conditions don't give true weightlessness, but it is the next best thing.

The training plane is nicknamed the "vomit comet"

Astronaut inside the tank trains for a spacewalk

Astronauts are weightless for about 25 seconds at a time inside the aircraft

► EFFECT ON THE BODY

Astronauts are monitored while in space to find out how weightlessness is affecting them. Nearly all astronauts experience some form of space sickness such as headache, nausea, and vomiting during the first day or two of weightlessness. Other effects last the duration of the space trip. Gravity isn't pulling on the body or its fluids and so astronauts have stuffy noses and puffy faces, and the heart doesn't have to pump so hard to send the blood round the body. Muscles weaken because they don't have to work so hard in weightless conditions, and calcium is lost from bones, making them weaker, too.

Gennady Padalka uses an ultrasound machine to study the effects of weightlessness on Mike Finke's body

MAN ON THE MOON

In total, 24 astronauts have traveled as far as the Moon, and 12 of them have walked on its surface. All 24 were men and from the U.S. They traveled in nine separate Apollo missions. The first missions tested the Apollo craft. Then, in December 1968, Apollo 8 orbited the Moon ten times, and five months later Apollo 10 approached its surface. The first mission to land astronauts on the Moon was Apollo 11 in July 1969.

Apollo 11
Neil Armstrong

Apollo 11
Buzz Aldrin

◄ SATURN V ROCKET

The astronauts started their journeys aboard Saturn V rockets, which launched from Cape Canaveral, Florida. The Apollo craft carrying the crew of three astronauts was in the nose cone of the rocket. Once above Earth, the Apollo craft was released to continue on to the Moon. The Saturn V is the largest rocket to fly successfully.

Apollo 15
David Scott

Apollo 15
James Irwin

Cone-shaped Command Module attached to drum-shaped Service Module with engine

▲ COMMAND AND SERVICE MODULES

The Apollo craft consisted of three parts—the Command Module, the Service Module, and the Lunar Module. The crew lived in the Command Module as they traveled to and from the Moon. Once at the Moon, two astronauts landed in the Lunar Module, while the third orbited the Moon in the combined Command and Service Modules. The Command Module was the only part to return to Earth.

Saturn V was 363 ft (111 m) high, as tall as a 30-story building

Apollo 12
Charles Conrad

Apollo 12
Alan Bean

Apollo 14
Alan Shepard

Apollo 14
Edgar Mitchell

Apollo 16
John Young

Apollo 16
Charles Duke

Apollo 17
Eugene Cernan

Apollo 17
Harrison Schmitt

◀MOONWALKERS

The 12 astronauts who walked on the Moon traveled there in six separate missions. The first was Neil Armstrong on July 21, 1969. Harrison Schmitt was the last onto the Moon, but Eugene Cernan was the last to step off, on December 14, 1972. In total, the astronauts spent more than 300 hours on the Moon's surface, 80 of which were outside their craft. Two Apollo 13 astronauts were also scheduled to land, but a fault in their craft meant they only traveled around the Moon before heading home.

◀APOLLO 11

Millions of people around the world watched on their TVs as the Apollo 11 astronauts explored the Moon. As Neil Armstrong took his first step on to its surface, he declared, "That's one small step for man; one giant leap for mankind." He was joined by Buzz Aldrin 19 minutes later. They collected 48.4 lb (22 kg) of rock and soil samples, took photographs, and set up equipment to detect moonquakes and measure the Earth–Moon distance.

▼LUNAR MODULE AND ROVER

The astronauts landed on the Moon's surface in the Lunar Module—the Apollo 11 module was called *Eagle*. The upper part was home while on the Moon, and this returned them to the rest of the orbiting Apollo craft once their work was complete.

The Lunar Modules of Apollos 15, 16, and 17 carried Lunar Roving Vehicles. These lightweight electric cars were used for exploring the lunar surface.

Lunar Module

Rover carried two astronauts, their tools, and rock samples that had been collected

Lower part of the module became a launch platform

Lunar Roving Vehicle

The space-suited astronauts found that kangaroo-style hops were the best way to move around

SPACESUIT

Astronauts wear a range of clothes in space—the different garments are designed for the variety of activities they do. Clothes include a suit worn during launch, casual clothes worn inside their craft while in space, and the white spacesuit worn by the astronauts who venture outside. Whatever the garment, it is designed with protection and comfort in mind. A spacesuit protects an astronaut from the space environment and lasts for about 25 spacewalks. The suits are kept in space, where they are adjusted to fit different astronauts.

Mission badge

▶ EXTRA-VEHICULAR SUIT
The spacesuit completely covers an astronaut's body and gives the astronaut their own Earthlike environment. The outer layer is a blend of waterproof, bulletproof, and fire-resistant fabric. A further seven layers make the suit act like a thermos flask and prevent temperature change inside. Further layers are tear resistant, hold in the oxygen, and maintain the proper pressure.

Metal ring to attach boot

Clips for attaching tools

▲ BOOTS
The spacesuit boots fit on to the end of the cloth legs of the suit. An interlocking alumium ring connects the two. The depth of the ring used depends on the length of the astronaut's leg. Astronauts wearing these boots hover or float and do not put their feet down, and so the boots are soft. Those designed for Moon walking had silicon soles and stainless-steel uppers.

Communications head gear called a "Snoopy hat"

ACES SUIT ▼
The Advanced Crew Escape Suit (ACES) is a pressure suit worn during launch and return to Earth. Its bright orange flameproof material makes an astronaut easily visible in an emergency. Underneath, the astronaut wears long-sleeve and long-pant underwear lined with tubes of cooling water. The suit is worn with a helmet, gloves, leather boots, and a parachute.

Neck cuff to attach helmet

Straps for attaching parachute

Spacesuit comes in two pieces: pants and top

Leather boots

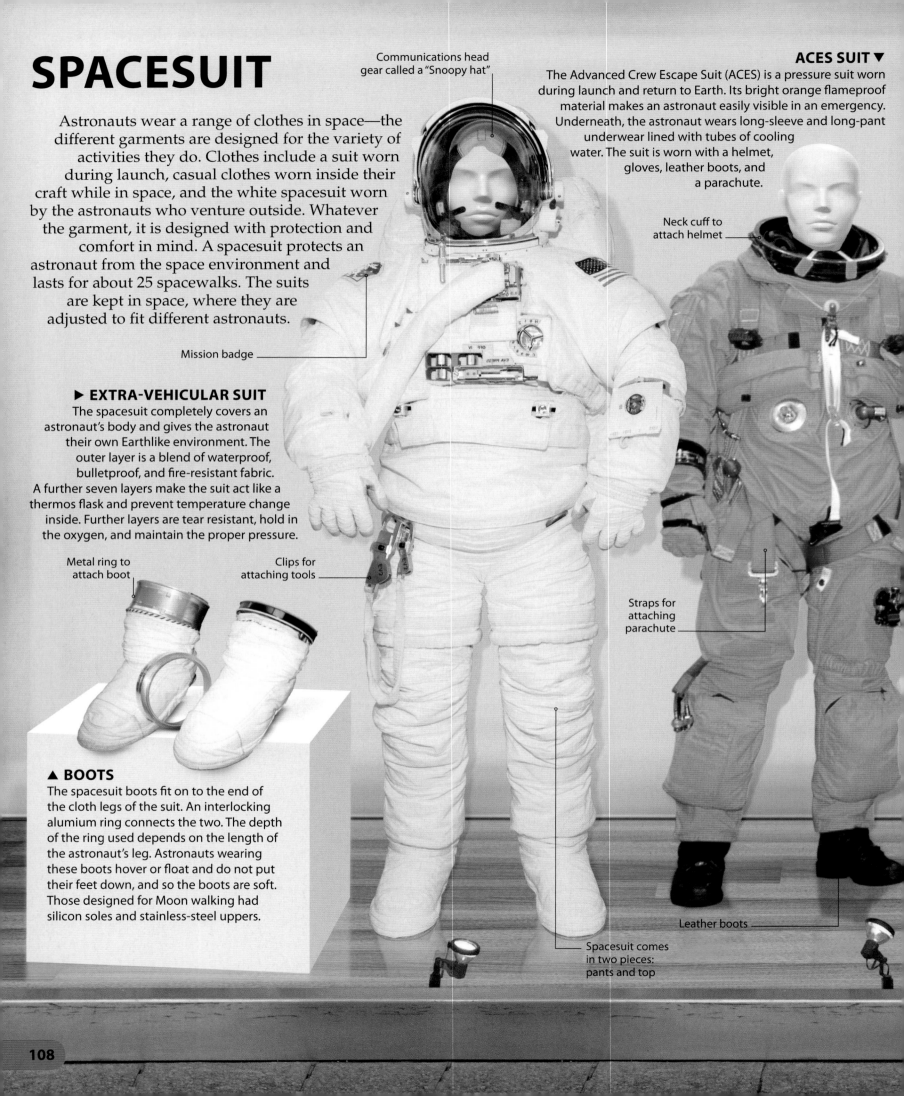

▼ HELMET

A hard-shelled helmet provides a protective pressurized environment for the astronaut's head. On the outside, a visor can be lowered to protect the face from the Sun's radiation. Inside, there is oxygen for breathing and a communication system.

◄ IN-FLIGHT SUIT

Some astronauts choose to wear in-flight suits when living in space. These one-piece suits that zip up the front are personalized with name badges and mission emblems. Zipper pockets on the suit's body, arms, and legs secure small items such as pens. Strips and squares of Velcro are also used to fix items down and prevent them floating away.

▼ CASUAL CLOTHES

Astronauts choose their casual clothes, such as polo-shirts, rugby-shirts, and loose pants or shorts, before launch. The mission emblem can be sewn onto them. Shirts and pants are changed on average every 10 days, underwear and socks every two days.

▲ EXERCISE CLOTHES

Each crew member onboard the International Space Station gets one pair of shorts and a T-shirt for every three days of exercising. They also get a pair of running shoes for the treadmill and another pair for the exercise bike. The dirty clothes are packed in a Progress supply vehicle, which burns up as it enters Earth's atmosphere.

Mission emblem

▲ GLOVES

Spacewalking astronauts use their hands as the main way to get around and for completing tasks. So their gloves need to be particularly comfortable and easy to use. The thumb and fingertips are moulded of silicone rubber for sensitivity. The astronauts control heaters in the fingertips to prevent their fingers from getting cold.

INTERNATIONAL SPACE STATION

The International Space Station (ISS) is a workplace and home for astronauts. It orbits Earth 15 times a day at an altitude of about 240 miles (390 km). The ISS is a collaboration of 16 countries: the U.S., Russia, Canada, Japan, 11 European countries, and Brazil. It was launched in parts, which were assembled in space.

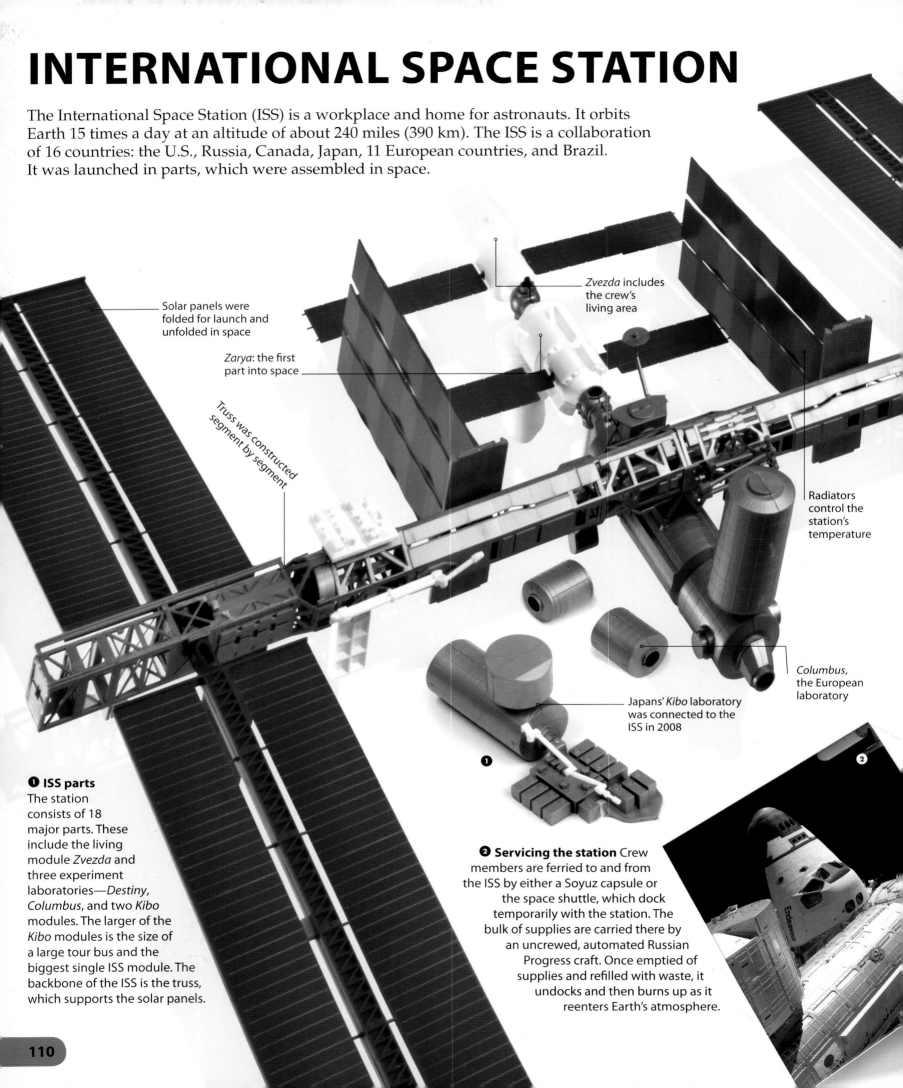

Solar panels were folded for launch and unfolded in space

Zarya: the first part into space

Truss was constructed segment by segment

Zvezda includes the crew's living area

Radiators control the station's temperature

Columbus, the European laboratory

Japans' *Kibo* laboratory was connected to the ISS in 2008

❶ ISS parts
The station consists of 18 major parts. These include the living module *Zvezda* and three experiment laboratories—*Destiny*, *Columbus*, and two *Kibo* modules. The larger of the *Kibo* modules is the size of a large tour bus and the biggest single ISS module. The backbone of the ISS is the truss, which supports the solar panels.

❷ Servicing the station Crew members are ferried to and from the ISS by either a Soyuz capsule or the space shuttle, which dock temporarily with the station. The bulk of supplies are carried there by an uncrewed, automated Russian Progress craft. Once emptied of supplies and refilled with waste, it undocks and then burns up as it reenters Earth's atmosphere.

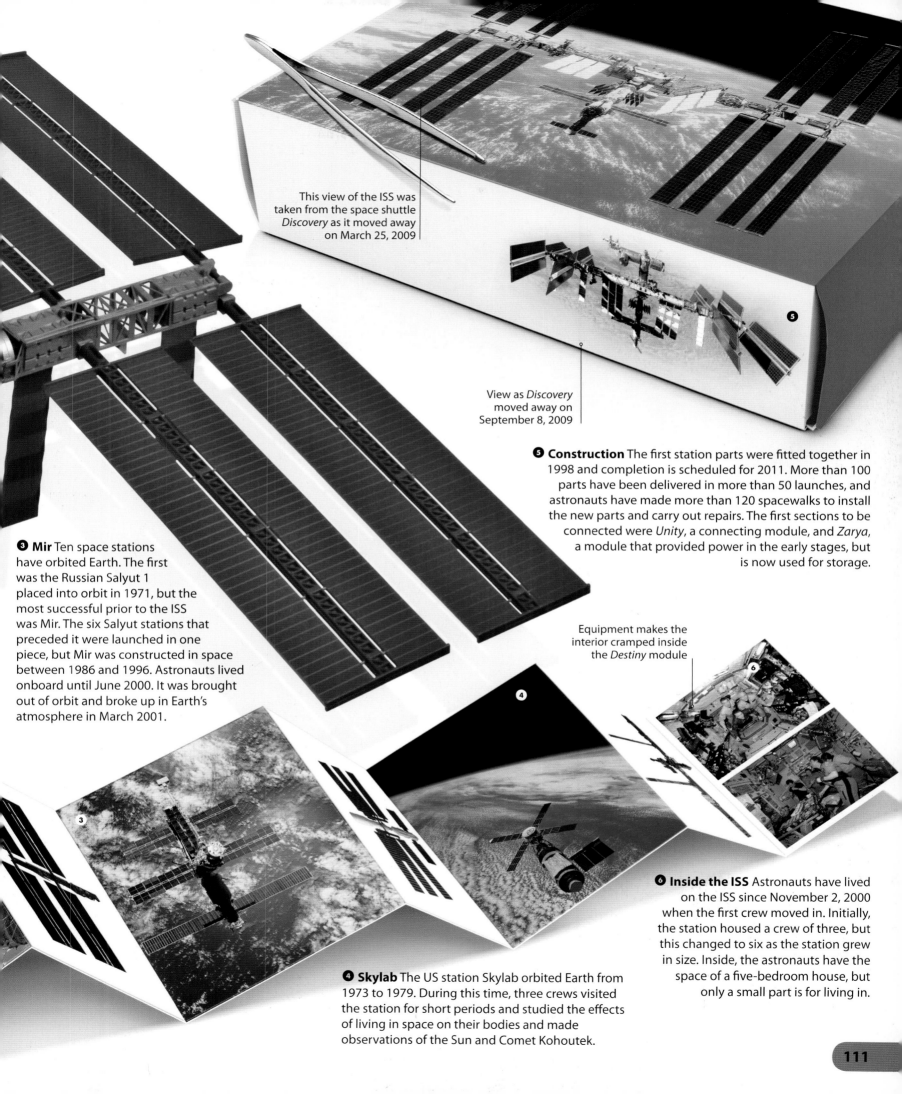

This view of the ISS was taken from the space shuttle *Discovery* as it moved away on March 25, 2009

View as *Discovery* moved away on September 8, 2009

❺ Construction The first station parts were fitted together in 1998 and completion is scheduled for 2011. More than 100 parts have been delivered in more than 50 launches, and astronauts have made more than 120 spacewalks to install the new parts and carry out repairs. The first sections to be connected were *Unity*, a connecting module, and *Zarya*, a module that provided power in the early stages, but is now used for storage.

❸ Mir Ten space stations have orbited Earth. The first was the Russian Salyut 1 placed into orbit in 1971, but the most successful prior to the ISS was Mir. The six Salyut stations that preceded it were launched in one piece, but Mir was constructed in space between 1986 and 1996. Astronauts lived onboard until June 2000. It was brought out of orbit and broke up in Earth's atmosphere in March 2001.

Equipment makes the interior cramped inside the *Destiny* module

❹ Skylab The US station Skylab orbited Earth from 1973 to 1979. During this time, three crews visited the station for short periods and studied the effects of living in space on their bodies and made observations of the Sun and Comet Kohoutek.

❻ Inside the ISS Astronauts have lived on the ISS since November 2, 2000 when the first crew moved in. Initially, the station housed a crew of three, but this changed to six as the station grew in size. Inside, the astronauts have the space of a five-bedroom house, but only a small part is for living in.

MISSION CONTROL

The International Space Station (ISS) is monitored around the clock. The people watching over it are based in a flight control room in Houston, Texas, and in another at the Mission Control Centre in Russia. They track the station, monitor the station's health and that of its crew, oversee operations, and provide backup when problems arise. Other centres in Germany, France, Canada, and Japan monitor the individual station parts built by those countries.

❶ CONTROL ROOM
The American ISS Flight Control Room is located at the Johnson Space Center in Houston, Texas. Recently refurbished, it was first used for space flight control in 1968 when Apollo 7, the first three-person American mission, was launched in preparation for later manned missions to the Moon. The staff, known as flight controllers, work in three teams, and each is on duty for about nine hours at a time.

❷ DISPLAY SCREENS

Huge screens at the front of the room provide up-to-date information on the station's position along its orbit. The TDRSS (Tracking and Data Relay Satellite System) is used to keep track of the station. It is a network of communication satellites positioned around Earth. Signals are received and transmitted by ground stations at White Sands, New Mexico, and at the Goddard Space Flight Center in Maryland.

❸ FLIGHT CONTROLLERS

About a dozen flight controllers work in the room at one time. Each has a specific function that they are assigned to. Each function has a particular call sign—the name they use when talking to other controllers. ROBO (Robotics Operations Systems Officer) watches over the station's robotic arm, and sitting behind is TITAN (Telemetry, Information Transfer, and Attitude Navigation).

❹ MISSION EMBLEMS

A wall of the control room is decorated by mission emblems. These are badges produced for manned and, less often, unmanned missions. The designs are unique to a mission and usually include the names of the mission and its crew. The emblems are produced as patches and worn on astronaut clothing.

❺ FLIGHT DIRECTOR

The seat next to the aisle on this console is taken by the flight director, the person in charge of the team presently working in the room. Next to the flight director is CAPCOM (Capsule Communicator), who speaks with the station crew on behalf of the Control Room. This role is often taken by an astronaut.

❻ EVA CONTROL

When the station astronauts make spacewalks, this console is occupied by the EVA (Extra-vehicular Activity) flight controller, who monitors the spacewalk and the spacesuits. Next to the EVA is the flight surgeon, who is responsible for the physical and psychological health and safety of the station's crew.

A DAY IN SPACE

Astronauts go to space to work, and like workers on Earth, they have set hours. Those aboard the International Space Station (ISS) work a five-day week and spend up to nine hours a day working. The rest of the time is spent doing normal human things, such as sleeping, eating, exercising, and personal hygiene. On their days off, astronauts have time to themselves, but they also spend time cleaning and repairing their space home.

1 6:00 A.M. BREAKFAST

A day on Earth is regulated by the position of the Sun in the sky. Astronauts can't use the Sun to help them—they see it rise about 16 times a day as they orbit Earth. A day is planned according to the time on their watches. It starts with a musical alarm call sent from Earth, which is then followed by breakfast.

2 7:00 A.M. PERSONAL HYGIENE

The astronauts clean themselves using wipes—one for washing and another for drying. Those staying on board for a short time wait to get home before washing their hair. Long-stay astronauts can clean their hair with rinseless shampoo. Teeth are cleaned using toothpaste that the astronauts swallow.

3 7:30 A.M. CONFERENCE

Before starting the working day, the astronauts gather together to discuss the schedule with the Flight Control Room on Earth. It is also a chance to report any problems encountered on the station and to pass on and receive messages from friends and family.

4 8:15 A.M. EXERCISE

Astronauts keep in shape by following a strict exercise routine. To prevent muscle loss, they each have two daily sessions on the space station's exercise equipment. The cycle machine strengthens their leg muscles. As the astronauts push against the pedals, straps hold them down to prevent them floating away.

5 10:30 A.M. WORK

Checklists explain in detail what the astronauts are required to do. Their work usually takes them to one of the laboratories, where they set up experiments or monitor those already under way. They also watch over experiments placed on platforms outside the ISS.

6 1:00 P.M. LUNCH

An astronaut's three daily meals are decided upon long before he or she goes into space. Favourite foods are then prepared and packaged. Some are ready to eat, whereas others need to have water added, while a small oven heats some meals.

7 2:00 P.M. WORK

Experiments in the ISS's *Kibo* laboratory include those on space medicine, biology, Earth observations, and material production. Here, an astronaut checks up on a crystal-growing experiment set up in the Protein Crystallization Research Facility rack.

8 5:00 P.M. EXERCISE

Astronauts have five main pieces of exercise equipment: two stationary bikes, two treadmills, and a piece of equipment that is similar to weight-lifting apparatus on Earth. A harness and straps hold the astronauts down on the treadmill.

9 6:00 P.M. WORK

Within the space station's *Columbus* laboratory module is an experiment facility known as the Microgravity Science Glovebox. It's a transparent mini-laboratory that the astronauts can put their gloved hands into. The sealed work area prevents small parts, fluids, or gases from escaping.

10 7:30 P.M. DINNER

Planned menus ensure that astronauts get the amount and type of food they individually need. Astronauts spending weeks or months at a time on the ISS have their meals repeated on a 10-day cycle. However, this diet is supplemented by fresh fruit, such as oranges, brought by astronauts joining them for a short stay.

11 8:30 P.M. CONFERENCE

The working day finishes with a run-through of the day's events with the Flight Control Room, and a preview of the plans for the following day. Every now and again, some of this conference time is also spent answering questions from the media. This is usually ahead of or after a spacewalk.

12 9:30 P.M. LEISURE TIME

The astronauts are now free from official duties and can enjoy moving and playing in the weightless environment. They can relax with a book, a DVD, or music, or they can get in touch with their families by laptop. A favorite pastime is gazing down on Earth and recording the view on camera.

13 10:00 P.M. SLEEP

Dressed in their daytime clothes or underwear, the astronauts settle down to sleep with or without a sleeping bag. An eye mask and ear plugs block out the light and noise. To prevent the astronauts floating around once they are asleep, arms are tucked in and the astronauts are fixed down.

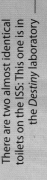
There are two almost identical toilets on the ISS. This one is in the *Destiny* laboratory

SPACEWALK

Astronauts who go outside their craft are said to be on extravehicular activity or EVA. This is more commonly known as a spacewalk. About 200 astronauts have made spacewalks: about two-thirds from the U.S., just over a third from Russia, and fewer than 20 from other countries. They wear a pressurized spacesuit that protects them from the space environment and supplies oxygen to breathe.

❶ FIRST SPACEWALK

Alexei Leonov made the first spacewalk on March 18, 1965 when he spent about ten minutes outside his Voskhod 2 craft. In that time his suit inflated and he found it difficult to re-enter. Once he released air from the suit, he squeezed back in through the hatch.

Astronauts Curbeam and Fuglesang work while flying high above New Zealand

❷ APOLLO SPACEWALKS

Nearly all spacewalks have been in Earth orbit. The exceptions are those made by Apollo astronauts on the Moon's surface and by three Apollo astronauts traveling back from the Moon. During a spacewalk lasting one hour and six minutes, Apollo 17 astronaut Ron Evans retrieved film from a camera positioned outside his craft as he returned to Earth in December 1972.

❸ WORKING OUTSIDE

In December 2006, Robert Curbeam and Christer Fuglesang (above) spent more than six hours installing a new part on the International Space Station. Astronauts have spent a total of about 800 hours working outside the station. Spacewalkers have to take all their tools with them. These are attached by strings that retract when the tool is not in use. Occasionally one drifts free and moves off on its own orbit around Earth.

❹ AIRLOCK
Astronauts spend about six hours preparing for a spacewalk. Much of this is in a small sealed room called an airlock. Here they get used to breathing oxygen and the different air pressure of their spacesuit. When ready to leave, air is pumped out of the airlock and the hatch is opened.

❺ TETHERED
During a spacewalk, an astronaut is secured to the craft. The first astronauts were attached by a tether that also supplied oxygen. Today, astronauts use ropelike tethers or are fixed by their feet and their back to the International Space Station's robotic arm.

❻ UNTETHERED
There have been fewer than 10 untethered spacewalks. In September 1994, Mark Lee tested the Simplified Aid for EVA Rescue (SAFER). This small backpack with thrusters is controlled from a chest-mounted unit and flies the astronaut back to safety if they mistakenly drift away.

Robot arm

❼ LONGEST SPACEWALK
Spacewalks regularly last up to seven hours. Susan Helms and Jim Voss set the record for the longest single spacewalk on March 11, 2001. They spent eight hours 56 minutes outside the International Space Station as they installed hardware to the external body of the *Destiny* module.

SPACE TOURIST

Until the start of the 21st century, the only way to travel into space was to enrol with a national space agency, complete astronaut training, and then hope to be selected to fly. Astronauts from many different countries continue to do this. Most are launched by Russia and the U.S., and a few by China. In recent years, however, a small number of people have flown aboard a Russian rocket as a private individual and paid for their trip into space.

❶ DENNIS TITO

The first person to pay for a trip into space was the American businessman Dennis Tito. He was the 415th person into space, but the first space tourist. The return trip in April 2001 cost him about US$20 million. He spent a week aboard the International Space Station (ISS), orbiting Earth 128 times.

❷ MARK SHUTTLEWORTH

Space tourists stay aboard the ISS alongside space agency astronauts. South African entrepreneur Mark Shuttleworth spent just over a week there in 2002. To make sure they don't jeopardize the trip for everyone, potential tourists undergo a minimum amount of astronaut training. For Shuttleworth, this included spending seven months at Star City, the Russian training center near Moscow.

❸ GREG OLSEN

The third space tourist was American scientist and entrepreneur Greg Olsen. Like all other space tourists, he was launched aboard a Russian Soyuz craft and stayed aboard the ISS. During his stay there in 2005, he became the subject of three experiments that tested the human body's response to the weightless environment. His most memorable part of the trip was floating around the ISS and watching the Earth pass by in the window.

❹ ANOUSHEH ANSARI

The only female space tourist was the Iranian-American engineer and businesswoman Anousheh Ansari. She stayed aboard the ISS in September 2006. She doesn't consider herself a tourist, but prefers the description "spaceflight participant" because she worked on the ISS. Like Olsen, Ansari was the subject of experiments, investigating astronaut's back pain, bacteria onboard the ISS, and the effects of radiation on the human body.

❺ CHARLES SIMONYI

When Hungarian-American Charles Simonyi spent time aboard the ISS in April 2007, he enjoyed the experience so much he decided to go again. The software developer made his second trip in April 2009. He stayed up at night to get the most from his time in space. He also gained an extra day in space because his return was delayed due to local ground conditions. In total, he spent nearly 27 days in space.

❻ RICHARD GARRIOTT

In October 2008, Richard Garriott became the sixth space tourist. More than any other, this video game developer was familiar with the life and work of an astronaut as his father, Owen Garriott, had lived aboard the Skylab space station for 60 days. On board the ISS, Richard Garriott photographed regions of the Earth. On his return, he compared his images to ones taken of the same area by his father 35 years previously.

❼ GUY LALIBERTÉ

Canadian circus entrepreneur Guy Laliberté returned to Earth on October 11, 2009, having spent 11 days in space. Like the previous six space tourists, his time had been spent inside the ISS. So far, no space tourist has spacewalked, but once space tourism becomes a regular part of space travel that could be the next step. Trips that take you to the Moon, round the back, and home again, may also become a real possibility.

❽ SPACESHIPTWO

Space tourism companies are already preparing their own craft and selling tickets for future space journeys. One of the first commercial spacecraft to make such flights will be SpaceShipTwo. After four days of preparation, its six passengers will travel 66 miles (110 km) above Earth, just beyond the edge of space. They will experience six minutes of weightlessness, during which they can release themselves from their seatbelts and float around the cabin. Their trip from launch to landing will last about two and a half hours.

SPACE TRANSPORT

Astronauts leave Earth and head for space on either a conventional rocket or in a rocket-powered space shuttle. Conventional rockets are used only once. The astronauts sit in their own small craft within the rocket's nose. On completion of their mission, the astronauts return home in the part of their craft that parachutes to Earth. By contrast, the shuttle is a reusable system that launches like a rocket and returns like a glider.

Upper part is adapted for each launch to take up to three satellites

Astronauts travel inside Soyuz-TMA craft inside nose

◄ SOYUZ FG

Soyuz rockets have been used to launch Russian astronauts since the 1960s. The Soyuz FG version now transports astronauts from a number of countries as well as space tourists on the first part of their journey to the International Space Station (ISS). Once released from the rocket, the craft containing the astronauts moves off to dock with the station.

First stage used five engines, which at launch consumed 15 tons of fuel per second

Third stage of the rocket

SATURN V ►

The Apollo astronauts who traveled to the Moon started their journey on board a Saturn V rocket. Saturn V's first two stages lifted the rocket and its cargo off the ground. The third stage moved the Apollo craft and its astronauts into Earth orbit. Then, after several orbits around Earth, the third stage set them on course for the Moon. Saturn V was the largest rocket ever used.

▲ ARIANE 5

The European rocket Ariane 5 was designed to carry both astronauts and spacecraft. So far, more than 40 Ariane 5s have launched, but none has carried humans. The rocket consists of two solid-fuel rocket boosters attached to either side of the two-stage central core. The first Ariane 5 launched the XMM-Newton space telescope, in 1999.

SPACE SHUTTLE ▼

The space shuttle system has three parts. First is the orbiter, the only part to go into space. Next is the orange fuel tank, which supplies fuel to the engines. Third are the two booster rockets, which help lift the system off the ground. The tank and boosters fall back to Earth soon after launch. Astronauts live on the orbiter or use it to travel to or from the ISS.

▲ ARES 1

Ares 1 is currently being developed to launch the Orion craft, which will take astronauts to the Moon. Ares 1 will replace the space shuttle on its retirement. In the years between the retirement and Ares 1's first manned flight, American astronauts will launch on board Russian Soyuz rockets.

SPACESHIPONE ▲

SpaceShipOne was the first privately owned piloted craft to travel to space more than once. In June 2004, Mike Melvill became the first commercial astronaut when he took the craft to 62 miles (100 km) above Earth—the edge of space. The White Knight aircraft carried SpaceShipOne to 9 miles (15 km) above Earth and then released it to ignite its rocket engines and move even higher.

Orbiter first carried astronauts to space in 1981

▶ LONG MARCH

Chinese astronauts are launched into space by a Long March 2F rocket. The astronauts are inside their Shenzhou craft, which consists of three modules. Once they have completed their orbits of Earth, they return home in the middle Shenzhou module. The Long March 2F launched China's first astronaut into space on October 15, 2003.

Four booster rockets provide thrust to lift off the launch pad

FUTURE JOURNEYS

Astronauts continue to spend time on board the ISS, but preparations are being made for them to travel to more distant destinations. Both the U.S. and China have plans to send astronauts to the Moon in the decades ahead, followed by Mars. A three-week stay on Mars would mean a round trip of 18 months and would be a challenge to the astronauts. The opportunity to travel in space will also become more widely available to private individuals, and in a few decades, it may be possible to holiday on the Moon.

The rover's living module allows astronauts to travel far from base

❶ ORION
The Orion spacecraft is scheduled to be the new transport vehicle for U.S. astronauts. Launched by an Ares 1 rocket, it will take over the space shuttle's role of delivering crew to the ISS from 2014. Further into the future, it will carry six astronauts at a time to the Moon. A lander module will separate from Orion and deliver them to the lunar surface. Then, after a stay of up to six months, Orion will return them home.

❷ LUNAR ROVER
Once on the Moon, the astronauts will be based in a fixed living module. A lunar rover will be one of a fleet of vehicles that will transport the astronauts as they explore the Moon's surface. The prototype rover is already being tested on Earth, on terrain similar to the Moon's surface. Travelling at about 6.2 mph (10 kph), the real thing will support a crew of two for up to 150 miles (240 km) from their base.

A robotic laboratory helps astronauts study the Martian surface

The prototype is 8.5 feet (2.6 m) wide— one-third the size of the planned final space hotel

❸ HUMANS ON MARS

The first planet that humans will visit will be Mars. The U.S. space agency has stated its intention to go there and their plan is to use the Orion craft to ferry astronauts to spacecraft assembled above Earth and waiting to carry the crews on to Mars. The first missions will be after the late 2030s and the journey to Mars will take about nine months.

❹ MARS 500

Space scientists are already assessing how a long space journey to Mars will affect any astronauts. Six volunteers spent 105 days in Mars 500, an isolation chamber in Moscow, Russia, during early 2009. Inside, they went through a series of scenarios as if traveling to Mars, including growing some of their own food and dealing with simulated emergencies.

❺ SPACE HOTEL

Private individuals can already book brief trips into space, but future generations might even be able to take a holiday in space. They will be able to stay aboard a space hotel that orbits Earth 16 times a day. A private organization has already tested its prototype space hotel, *Genesis 1*, in space. Launched by rocket from Russia, it inflated to twice its size once in orbit.

Glossary

ACTIVE GALAXY
A galaxy that emits an exceptional amount of energy, much of which comes from a supermassive black hole in its center.

ALIEN
A creature who comes from a world other than Earth.

ANTENNA
An aerial in the shape of a rod, dish, or array for receiving or transmitting radio waves.

ASTEROID
A small, rocky body orbiting the Sun. Most are in the Main Belt between Mars and Jupiter.

ASTRONAUT
A man or woman who travels into space.

ASTRONOMER
Someone who studies the stars, planets, and other objects in space.

ATMOSPHERE
The layer of gases held around a planet, moon, or star by its gravity.

ATOM
The smallest particle of a chemical element.

AURORA
A light display above a planet's polar region produced when particles hit atoms in the planet's atmosphere and make it glow.

BIG BANG
The explosive event that created the universe 13.7 billion years ago.

BILLION
One thousand million (1 followed by nine zeros).

BLACK HOLE
The remains of a star, or a galaxy core that has collapsed in on itself. A galactic black hole is often referred to as a supermassive black hole.

BRIGHTNESS
A measure of the light of a star. Astronomers measure brightness in two ways—as seen from Earth, and the amount of light a star emits.

CELL
The basic unit in all living things. A cell may exist as an independent unit of life, or many can combine to form complex tissue, as in plants and animals.

CLUSTER
A group of galaxies or stars held together by gravity.

COMET
A small snow and dust body. Those traveling near the Sun develop a head and two tails.

CONSTELLATION
An imaginary pattern made from stars and the region of sky around them. Earth's sky is divided into 88 different constellations.

CONVECTION
The transfer of heat by movement, for instance when warmer gas rises and cooler gas falls in a star.

COSMOLOGIST
A person who studies the origin, evolution, and future of the universe.

CRATER
A bowl-shaped hollow on the surface of a planet or moon, formed when an asteroid crashes into it.

DARK ENERGY
A mysterious form of energy that makes up 72 percent of the universe and is responsible for the acceleration of the expansion of the universe.

DARK MATTER
Matter that does not emit energy but whose gravity affects its surroundings. It makes up 23 percent of the universe.

DENSITY
A measure of how tightly the mass of an object is packed into its volume.

DWARF GALAXY
A small galaxy containing only a million to several billion stars.

DWARF PLANET
An almost round body that orbits the Sun as part of a belt of objects.

ECLIPSE
The effect achieved when one body, such as a star or planet, is in the shadow of another.

ELECTROMAGNETIC RADIATION
A range of energy waves that travel through space. They include gamma rays, X rays, ultraviolet, infrared, microwaves, visible light, and radio waves.

ELEMENT
A basic substance of nature, such as hydrogen or oxygen.

ELLIPTICAL
Shaped like an ellipse, which is an elongated circle or sphere.

EQUATOR
An imaginary line drawn around the middle of a planet, moon, or star, halfway between its north and south poles.

EXOPLANET
A planet that orbits around a star other than the Sun. Sometimes called an extrasolar planet.

EXTRATERRESTRIAL
Something or somebody that comes from somewhere other than Earth.

FLYBY
A close encounter made with a solar system object by a spacecraft that flies past without going onto orbit.

GALACTIC
Relating to a galaxy; for example, a "galactic nucleus" is the central part of a galaxy.

GALAXY
An enormous grouping of stars, gas, and dust held together by gravity.

GIANT PLANET
One of the four largest solar system planets. In order of decreasing size and distance from the Sun, they are Jupiter, Saturn, Uranus, and Neptune.

GRAVITY
A force of attraction found throughout the universe. The greater the mass of a body, the greater is its gravitational pull.

HELIUM
The second most abundant chemical element in the universe.

HYDROGEN
The lightest and most abundant chemical element in the universe.

KUIPER BELT OBJECT
A rock and ice body orbiting the Sun within the Kuiper Belt, beyond the orbit of Neptune.

LANDER
A spacecraft that lands on the surface of a planet, moon, asteroid, or comet.

LAVA
Molten rock released through a volcano or vent in the surface of a planet or moon.

LIGHT YEAR
A unit of distance. One light year is the distance light travels in one year—that is 5.88 million million miles (9.46 million million km).

LUMINOSITY
The total amount of energy emitted in one second by a star.

LUNAR
Relating to the Moon; for example, the "lunar surface" is the surface of the Moon.

MAGNETIC FIELD
Any place where a magnetic force can be measured, such as around Earth.

MAIN BELT
See asteroid.

MAIN SEQUENCE
A stage in the lifetime of a star, when the star shines by converting hydrogen into helium in its core. About 90 percent of stars are main sequence stars.

MARE (PLURAL MARIA)
A smooth plain of solidified lava on the Moon.

MASS
A measure of the amount of material (matter) a body is made of.

MATTER
The substance that things are made of.

METEOR
A short-lived streak of light produced by a small piece of comet speeding through Earth's upper atmosphere.

METEORITE
A piece of rock or metal that lands on a planet's or moon's surface; most are pieces of an asteroid.

MICROBIAL
Referring to a microorganism, a minute form of life.

MICROORGANISM
A tiny form of life, such as a bacterium, which is not visible to the naked eye.

MILKY WAY
The galaxy we live in. It is also, the name given to the band of stars that crosses Earth's sky and is our view into the galaxy's disk.

MILLION
The figure 1 followed by six zeros.

MODULE
A complete unit of a spacecraft; for instance, *Zvezda* is a module of the International Space Station.

MOON
A rock, or rock and ice, body that orbits a planet or an asteroid.

NEBULA (PLURAL NEBULAE)
A cloud of gas and dust in space. Some emit their own light, others shine by reflecting light, and those that block out light from background stars appear dark.

NEUTRON STAR
A dense, compact star formed from the core of an exploding star. It is about the size of a city but consists of the same mass as the Sun.

NUCLEAR REACTION
The process whereby elements inside a star produce other elements and energy is released; for instance, hydrogen nuclei fuse to produce helium, and energy such as heat and light is emitted in the process.

NUCLEUS (PLURAL NUCLEI)
The body of a comet, the central part of a galaxy, or the central core of an atom.

OORT CLOUD
A sphere consisting of more than a trillion comets that surrounds the planetary part of the solar system.

ORBIT
The path that a natural or artificial body makes around another more massive body.

ORBITER
A spacecraft that orbits around a space body, such as a planet or asteroid.

ORGANISM
An individual form of life such as a single-cell bacterium, an animal, or a plant.

PENUMBRA
The lighter, outer part of a shadow cast by a space body, and also the lighter and warmer, outer region of a sunspot.

PHOTOSPHERE
The outer, visible layer of the Sun, or another star.

PLANET
A massive, round body that orbits around a star and shines by reflecting the star's light.

PLANETARY NEBULA
A colorful expanding cloud of ejected gas and dust surrounding the remains of a dying star.

POLAR
Relating to the north and south poles of an object.

PRESSURE
The force felt when something presses against a surface.

PROTOSTAR
A very young star in the early stages of formation, before nuclear reactions start in its core.

PULSAR
A rapidly rotating neutron star from which we receive brief pulses of energy as the star spins.

RADIATION
Energy traveling as electromagnetic waves such as infrared or light.

ROCK PLANET
One of the four planets closest to the Sun and made of rock and metal. In order of distance from the Sun, they are Mercury, Venus, Earth, and Mars.

ROVER
A spacecraft that moves across the surface of a planet or moon.

SATELLITE
An artificial object deliberately placed in orbit around Earth or another solar system body. Also, another name for a moon or any space object orbiting a larger one.

SILICATE
Rocky material containing the elements silicon, oxygen, and one or more other common elements. Most rocks on Earth are silicates.

SOLAR
Relating to the Sun; for example, the "solar temperature" is the temperature of the Sun.

SOLAR SYSTEM
The Sun and the objects that orbit it, including the planets and many smaller bodies.

SPACESUIT
The all-in-one sealed clothing unit worn by astronauts when outside their craft in space.

SPACEWALK
An excursion by an astronaut outside a craft when in space.

SPECTROGRAPH
An instrument that splits energy, such as light, into its component wavelengths. These wavelengths are then analyzed to reveal an object's properties.

SPECTRUM
The rainbow band of colors that is produced when light is split.

STAR
A huge sphere of hot, luminous gas that generates energy by nuclear reactions.

SUPERCLUSTER
A grouping of galaxy clusters held together by gravity.

SUPERGIANT
An exceptionally large and luminous star.

SUPERNOVA (PLURAL SUPERNOVAE)
A star that explodes and leaves a supernova remnant behind, and whose core can become a neutron star, pulsar, or black hole.

TRILLION
One million million (1 followed by 12 zeros).

UMBRA
The dark, inner shadow cast by a space body. Also, the darker, cooler inner region of a sunspot.

UNIVERSE
Everything that exists; all space and everything in it.

VOLUME
The amount of space an object occupies.

WAVELENGTH
The distance between the peaks or troughs in waves of energy.

WEIGHTLESSNESS
The sensation experienced by astronauts in space because traveling in space is like constantly falling through space.

ZODIAC
The band of 12 constellations that form the background to the Sun, Moon, and planets as they move across the sky.

Index

Acknowledgments

DK would like to thank:
Richard Ferguson for paper engineering, Guy Harvey for the model-making, the Apple Agency for the artwork on pp90–91, Rich Cando for the artwork on pp114–115, and Chris Bernstein for preparing the index.

The publisher would like to thank the following for their kind permission to reproduce their photographs:

Key: a–above; b–below/bottom; c–center; f–far; l–left; r–right; t–top

1–5: **CNES, ESA, European Southern Observatory (ESO) & NASA. 6–7 NASA:** ESA / Hubble SM4 ERO Team. **8 European Southern Observatory (ESO):** M. McCaughrean & M. Andersen (AIP) (c/stage 4: Pillars of Creation). **NASA:** Hubble Heritage Team (AURA / STScI / NASA) (c/stage 5: Dusty Spiral Galaxy NGC 4414); JPL-Caltech / E. Churchwell (University of Wisconsin-Madison) / GLIMPSE Team (fbr/stage 5: Black Widow Nebula); JPL-Caltech / SSC / Harvard-Smithsonian CfA (c/stage 5: Spiral Galaxy M81); JPL-Caltech / SSC (cra/stage 5: Spiral Galaxy NGC 1365); JPL-Caltech / University of Wisconsin (fcra/stage 5: RCW 49 Nebula); Hubble Image: NASA, ESA, K. Kuntz (JHU), F. Bresolin (University of Hawaii), J. Trauger (Jet Propulsion Lab), J. Mould (NOAO), Y.-H. Chu (University of Illinois, Urbana), & STScI / CFHT Image: Canada-France-Hawaii Telescope / J.-C. Cuillandre / Coelum / NOAO Image: G. Jacoby, B. Bohannan, M. Hanna & NOAO / AURA / NSF (c stage 5: Spiral Galaxy Messier 101); N.A. Sharp / AURA / NOAO / NSF (cra/stage 5: Starburst Galaxy M82). **8–9 Corbis:** Bettman (c/stage 5: more Andromeda Galaxy); Stocktrek Image (c/stage 5: Andromeda Galaxy); Stocktrek Images (c/stage 5: Andromeda Galaxy) (c/stage 4: tapestry of galaxies from the Hubble Ultra Deep Field); A. A. Aloisi (Space Telescope Science Institute & European Space Agency, Baltimore, Md.) (c/stage 5: I Zwicky 18); ESA / Hubble Heritage Team (STScI / AURA) / J. Blakeslee (JHU) / R. Thompson (University of Arizona) (c/stage 4: galaxies); ESA / Hubble Heritage Team (STScI / AURA) / M. Mountain (STScI) / P. Puxley (NSF) / J. Gallagher (University of Wisconsin) (c/stage 5: M82); ESA / J. Blakeslee & H. Ford (Johns Hopkins University) (c/stage 4: more galaxies); ESA / M. Livio (STScI) & Hubble Heritage Team (STScI / AURA) (c/stage 5: Galaxy Triplet Arp 274); ESA / S. Beckwith (STScI) / HUDF Team (c/stage 4: earliest galaxies). **NASA:** ESA / M. Roberto (Space Telescope Science Institute / ESA) / Hubble Space Telescope Orion Treasury Project Team (c/stage 3: Orion Nebula); JPL-Caltech / CfA (c/stage 3: Christmas Tree Cluster); C.R. O'Dell & S.K. Wong (Rice University) (c/stage 3: Great Orion Nebula). **Science Photo Library:** Victor De Schwanberg (cl/stage 1: Big Bang). **9 NASA:** (fclb/stage 5: Milky Way); ESA / S. Beckwith (STScI) / Hubble Heritage Team (STScI / AURA) (cla/stage 5: Whirlpool Galaxy & Companion Galaxy); Hubble Heritage Team (AURA / STScI) / S. Smartt (Institute of Astronomy) / D. Richstone (University of Michigan) (fcla/stage 5: Black Eye Galaxy M64) (clb/stage 5: Galaxy M101); JPL / California Institute of Technology (c/stage 5: Andromeda Galaxy); JPL-Caltech (cla/stage 5: Triangulum Galaxy); WMAP Science Team (tl/stage 5: Barred Spiral Galaxy NGC1365). **10 Getty Images:** NASA (3/br). **iStockphoto.com:** Timothy Boomer (tr/cookie); Bruce Lonngren (tl/napkin). **NASA:** K. Sharon (Tel Aviv University) / E. Ofek (Caltech) (2/bl); NASA, CXC, CfA & D. Evans et al. (X-ray) / NASA & STScI (Optical/UV) / NSF, VLA, CfA & D.Evans et al. (Radio) / TFC, JBO & MERLIN (1/cl) (table cloth background). **10–11 iStockphoto.com:** book pages). **11 Dreamstime.com:** Iurii Konoval (br/pen & cup of coffee). **iStockphoto.com:** Robyn Mackenzie (fcbr/coffee stain). **NASA:** JPL-Caltech / Institut d'Astrophysique Spatiale (5/fclb); JPL / Space Science Institute (7/bl). **Science Photo Library:** Celestial Image Co. (4/ftl); U.S. Geological Survey (6/cb). **12–13 Getty Images:** Jason Hindley / Photonica (window background). **NASA:** ESA / S. Beckwith (STScI) / HUDF Team (1). **13 iStockphoto.com:** Steffen Hoejager (tl/picture frame). **Max-Planck-Institut für Astrophysik:** Volker Springel (2/tl/ framed image). **14 Corbis:** NASA / JPL-Caltech / SOHO / Extreme Ultraviolet Imaging Telescope (EIT) consortium (5/ ca). **iStockphoto.com:** (bl). **NASA:** A. Feild (Space Telescope Science Institute) (8/fcrb); Hubble Heritage Team (STScI / AURA) / R.G. French (Wellesley College) / J. Cuzzi (NASA / Ames) / L. Dones (SwRI) / J. Lissauer (NASA / Ames) (6/tr); R. Hurt (SSC-Caltech) / JPL-Caltech (7/cr); JPL (4/tc). **Science Photo Library:** Russell Croman (3/cla); NOAA (2/fcla). **14–15 Dreamstime.com:** Paul Maguire (background). **iStockphoto.com:** (fabric swatch shapes). **15 Corbis:** Tony Hallas / Science Faction (br/bl); Stocktrek Images (11/cb). **iStockphoto.com:** Heike Kampe (tr). **NASA:** CXC / SAO (9/fcla); ESA / P. van Dokkum (Yale University) / M. Franx (Leiden University, The Netherlands) / G. Illingworth (University of California, Santa Cruz, & Lick Observatory) (13/crb). **Science Photo Library:** Celestial Image Co. (12/bc). **16 Canada-France-Hawaii Telescope:** Coelum. Image by Jean-Charles Cuillandre (CFHT) & Giovanni Anselmi (Coelum) (1/l). **NASA:** JPL-Caltech / University of Arizona (2/br). **16–17 Alamy Images:** Antiques & Collectables (glass globes). **17 NASA:** ESA / CFHT / NOAO / K. Kuntz (GSFC) / F. Bresolin (University of Hawaii) / J. Trauger (JPL) / J. Mould (NOAO) / Y.-H. Chu (University of Illinois) (3/cl); ESA / Hubble Heritage Team (AURA / STScI) (4/br); Hubble Heritage Team (AURA / STScI / NASA) (5/cra). **18 Corbis:** NASA / Hubble Heritage / Digital / Science Faction / Encyclopedia (br/Arp 272). **Getty Images:** NASA / Stocktrek Images (tr/ Antennae). **NASA:** H. Fort (JHU) / G. Illingworth (USCS & LO) / M. Clampin (STScI) & G. Hartig (STScI) / ACS Science Team / ESA (cl/Mice); Hubble Heritage Team (AURA / STScI) (tc/Black Eye); STScI (bl/Cartwheel). **18–19 iStockphoto.com:** Hilary Seselja (star shapes background); ESA / Hubble Heritage Team (STScI / AURA) ESA & Hubble Collaboration / A. Evans (University of Virginia, Charlottesville, & NRAO / Stony Brook University) (cl/UGC 8335). **19 NASA:** ESA / P. van Dokkum (Yale University) / M. Franx (Leiden University, The Netherlands) / G. Illingworth (University of California, Santa Cruz, & Lick Observatory) (bl/early galaxies). **20 NASA:** CXC, CfA, R. Kraft et al. / MPIfR, ESO, APEX, A. Weiss et al. (submillimeter) / ESO & WFI (optical) (1/tl); ESA / ESO /

Frédéric Courbin (École Polytechnique Fédérale de Lausanne) / Pierre Magain (Université de Liège) (2/tr). **20–21 Getty Images:** Comstock (background). **21 NASA:** Hubble Heritage Team (AURA / STScI / NASA) (4/tr). **Science Photo Library:** Jodrell Bank (3/cl). **22 NASA:** JPL-Caltech / R. Hurt (SSC) (2/ cra). **Science Photo Library:** Chris Butler (3/cr). **22–23 Getty Images:** Paul & Lindamarie Ambrose (1/t); Frank Whitney (cinema drive). **23 iStockphoto.com:** Paul Rosado (5/br/road sign). **NASA:** CXC / MIT / F.K.Baganoff et al. (4/cla). **24 Photolibrary:** Bernd Vogel / Fancy (b/unwrapped chocolate). **24–25 Alamy Images:** Food Features (other wrapped-up chocolates). **25 Alamy Images:** David J. Green - studio (chocolates tin). **NASA:** ESA / Hubble Heritage Team (STScI / AURA) / Y. Momany (University of Padua) (7/bc); JPL-Caltech / R. Hurt (SSC) (1/tl); JPL-Caltech (3/cl). **NOAO / AURA / NSF:** (4/c); Local Group Galaxies Survey Team (6/clb); Bill Schoening / Vanessa Harvey / REU program / T. Rector & B.A. Wolpa (2/cra); S. Van Dyk (IPAC / Caltech) et al. / KPNO 2.1-m Telescope (8/br). **Science Photo Library:** Royal Observatory, Edinburgh / AATB (5/tr). **26–27 NOAO / AURA / NSF:** T.A. Rector (NRAO / AUI / NSF and NOAO / AURA / NSF) and B.A. Wolpa (NOAO / AURA / NSF, x). **28 iStockphoto.com:** (cb/billboard); Michal Gach (l/billboard). **NASA:** ESA / E. Olszewski (University of Arizona) (tl/star cluster). **28–29 Corbis:** Roger Ressmeyer (t/starry sky). **iStockphoto.com:** (cb/ billboard); Alexander Hafemann (b/city skyline background). **Science Photo Library:** Mark Garlick (cla/star size). **29 Corbis:** Roger Ressmeyer (tl/star luminosity). **iStockphoto.com:** (billboard 1 & 2). **NASA:** STEREO / Naval Research Laboratory (cr/sun). **30 Dreamstime.com:** Dmitry Rukhlenko (l/sun and blue sky). **NASA:** Goddard Space Flight Center, Scientific Visualization Studio (2/fbr); Hinode JAXA / PPARC (1/br). **30–31 Alamy Images:** R. Frank / Arco Images (c/postcard stand). **Corbis:** Jim Jurica (beach background). **31 Corbis:** Skylab / NRL / NASA / Roger Ressmeyer / Terra (4/bc). **NASA:** JPL-Caltech / NRL / GSFC (3/bl). **Science Photo Library:** Philippe Plailly / Eurelios (3/cr). **32 Corbis:** M. Robberto (Space Telescope Science Institute / ESA) and the Hubble Space Telescope Orion Treasury Project Team / NASA / ESA / Terra (2/tr). **European Southern Observatory (ESO):** (1/cl/Horsehead Nebula). **32–33 Corbis:** R. Creation / Amanaimages (windchime and sky); Space Telescope Wide Field and Planetary Camera 2 / Bettmann (3/c). **33 NASA:** ESA / N. Smith (University of California, Berkeley) / The Hubble Heritage Team (STScI / AURA) for the Hubble image & N. Smith (University of California, Berkeley) & NOAO / AURA / NSF for the CTIO Image (4/cl); ESA / M. Livio (STScI) (5/cr). **Copyright © Subaru Telescope, National Astronomical Observatory of Japan (NAOJ). All right reserved.:** (6/br). **34 Corbis:** Stocktrek Images (tl/Pleiades), **Science Photo Library:** Celestial Image Co. (clb/Butterfly Cluster). **34–35 Corbis:** Imagemore Co., Ltd (lantern flying scene). **35 Corbis:** Mark Garlick, Words & Pictures Ltd / Science Photo Library (br/close pair); Stocktrek Images (cl/globular cluster). **Science Photo Library:** John Chumack (cla/companions). **36 Corbis:** Frans Lanting (1/cla); Space Telescope Faint Object Camera / Bettmann (3/bl). **NASA:** ESA / G. Bacon (STScI) (4/cb). **Science Photo Library:** John Sanford (cla). **36–37 iStockphoto.com:** Igor Kalioujny (large round diamond shapes). **Photolibrary:** Vstock, LLC (rings background). **37 Corbis:** NASA / JPL-Caltech (8/bc). **NASA:** Y. Chu (UIUC) et al. & NASA –X-ray / J. P. Harrington & K. J. Borkowski (UMD) –Optical / Z. Levay (STScI) –Composite (6/clb); JPL (Raghvendra Sahai) (7/ cra); Space Telescope Science Institute (5/tr). **38 Corbis:** Mehau Kulyk / Science Photo Library (cb); Stocktrek Images / Corbis Yellow (3/crb) (cl/sad emoticon). **iStockphoto.com:** (bc/smiley); Patrick A. Krost (cr/star badge). **Science Photo Library:** Mark Garlick (2/cb). **38–39 iStockphoto.com:** Laryn Bakker (front of canopy & metal posts); Ron Sumners (t-shirts). **39 Getty Images:** Stocktrek Images (4/clb) (br/ power button). **iStockphoto.com:** (c/recycle logo); Patrick A. Krost (bl/star button). **NASA:** J. Hester / Arizona state University (5/bc). **40 ESA:** / Hubble, NASA & P. Kalas (University of California, Berkeley) (2/clb/Fomalhaut). **European Southern Observatory (ESO) :** (1/clb). **NASA:** ESA / D. Lafrenière (University of Toronto) (3/clb). **40–41 Corbis:** Mark McCaughrean (Max-Planck-Institute for Astronomy) / C. Robert O'Dell (Rice University) / NASA (4/bc). **Getty Images:** Lorenz & Avelar / Workbook Stock (b/control board). **iStockphoto.com:** Andrey Prokhorov (bc/radar). **41 European Southern Observatory (ESO) :** (5/t). **42 iStockphoto.com:** Nick Schlax (br/pencil). **42–43 iStockphoto.com:** (background). **43 Corbis:** Roger Ressmeyer (cr/Ursa Major constellation). **iStockphoto.com:** Monika Adamczyk (b/pencil case); Konstantin Kirillov (tr/ paint and brushes); Nick Schlax (clb/pencils). **44–45 NASA:** JPL / USGS. **46 Corbis:** Denis Scott (2/crb). **Getty Images:** NASA (4/crb/asteroid Eros). **NASA:** JPL (3/crb); JPL (6/crb/Ida); JPL / University of Arizona (7/cb); SOHO (1/fcrb); USGS (4/crb). **Science Photo Library:** California Association for Research in Astronomy (9/bl). **46–47 iStockphoto.com:** Ermin Gutenberger (background). **47 iStockphoto.com:** Nicholas (cr). **NASA:** ESA / A. Feild (STScI) (11/ca); JPL (clb/Gaspra) (5/ clb) (8/clb) (10/br). **Science Photo Library:** Friedrich Saurer (11/cla/Eris). **48 NASA:** JPL (2/cr); JPL (3/tr). **48–49 NASA:** JPL (4/c). **Greg Robbins:** (globe background) (c/globe stand). **49 Getty Images:** Jupiterimages / Thinkstock (c/globe stand). **NASA:** JPL / NASA Goddard Space Flight Center Image by Reto Stöckli (land surface, shallow water, clouds) / Enhancements by Robert Simmon (ocean color, compositing, 3D globes, animation) / Data and technical support: MODIS Land Group, MODIS Science Data Support Team, MODIS Atmosphere Group, MODIS Ocean Group Additional data by USGS EROS Data Center (topography), USGS Terrestrial Remote Sensing Flagstaff Field Center (Antarctica) & Defense Meteorological Satellite Program (city lights) (5/c). **50 Corbis:** NASA / Bettmann (2/crb). **Science Photo Library:** Joe Tucciarone (bl); Detlev Van Ravenswaay (cb). **50–51 NASA:** JPL / Cornell (Mars background). **51 Corbis:** NASA / Science Faction (fbl/Mercury craters). **NASA:** JPL-Caltech / University of Arizona / Cornell / Ohio State University (br). **Science Photo Library:** Planetobserver (cb). **52 Alamy Images:** Phil Degginger (l/br). **Corbis:** NASA / Roger Ressmeyer (3/tr). **52–53 iStockphoto.com:** Andrea Hill (fireworks & night's sky); Andrzej Tokarski

(horizontal firework rockets). **53 Corbis:** NASA - JPL / Roger Ressmeyer (4/fbr). **Dreamstime.com:** Marius Droppert (cr/ fireworks rocket with golden top); Jostein Hauge (tr/yellow/ pink rocket). **iStockphoto.com:** Achim Prill (r/conic fountains); Damir Spanic (r/lawn background). **NASA:** JPL (5/ cra). **Photolibrary:** Guido Alberto Rossi / Tips Italia (2/br). **Science Photo Library:** Mark Garlick (6/tr). **54 Getty Images:** Daniele Pellegrini / The Image Bank (1/tr). **NASA:** JPL / MSSS (2/cr). **54–55 Getty Images:** Dimitri Vervitsiotis / Digital Vision (umbrellas & rain background). **55 ESA:** DLR / FU Berlin (G. Neukum) (3/fcla). **Getty Images:** Georgette Douwma / Photographer's Choice (5/r). **NASA:** JPL (4/bl). **56 Corbis:** Roger Ressmeyer (tc). **Getty Images:** Stocktrek Images (clb/ lunar soil image). **iStockphoto.com:** Vladislav Sukoy (ftl). **56–57 iStockphoto.com:** (c/desktop calendar). **57 Alamy Images:** Archives du 7ème Art / Photos 12 (tc). **FLPA:** Erica Olsen (bc) (cr). **Science Photo Library:** Eckhard Slawik (l/ phases of the Moon). **58 CNES:** Jean-Pierre Haigneré, 1999 (clb/shadow on the Earth). **Science Photo Library:** Rev. Ronald Royer (cla/solar eclipse). **58–59 Dorling Kindersley:** Judith Miller / Biddle & Webb of Birmingham (b/desk); Science Museum, London (c/orrery). **iStockphoto.com:** (gilded picture frames). **59 Alamy Images:** Papilio (tl/eclipse). **Rahu Om Chan Singapore:** (cb/Rahu). **Science Photo Library:** G. Antonio Milani (cr/red moon); David Nunuk (tr/ rings and beads). **60 Getty Images:** JAXA / AFP (2/cb). **iStockphoto.com:** Matt Schmitz (tl). **NASA:** JPL (1/cb); JPL (3/cra). **60–61 Dreamstime.com:** Les Palenik (cl/TV frame). **NASA:** JPL (4/cb). **61 iStockphoto.com:** Andrew Manley (r). **NASA:** NEAR Spacecraft Team / JHUAPL (5/ftl) (fcla/small balloon). **62 Alamy Images:** Chuck Pefley (cb/small balloon). **Dreamstime.com:** Sonya Etchison (tr/jupiter balloon). **iStockphoto.com:** Sarah Holmstrom (br/hot-air balloon); Jacom Stephens (cl/hot-air balloon). **NASA:** Reta Beebe & Amy Simon (New Mexico State Univ.) (tr/Jupiter planet); JPL (cl/Saturn planet); JPL / Space Science Institute (br/planet cross-section). **62–63 Getty Images:** Digital Vision (background) (cb/small hot-air balloon). **63 Alamy Images:** Chuck Pefley (2/cb). **Dreamstime.com:** Sherri Camp (tr/hot-air balloon); Jeffrey Banke (bl/hot-air balloon). **iStockphoto.com:** Jacom Stephens (br/hot-air balloon). **NASA:** JPL (br/Neptune). **Science Photo Library:** California Association For Research In Astronomy (cla/Herschel); Royal Astronomical Society (cra/Galle). **64 iStockphoto.com:** David Morgan (bc/frame); Lisa F. Young (c/weatherman). **NASA:** JPL (2/tr) (3/bc). **64–65 iStockphoto.com:** (TV); Bill Noll (wallpaper background); Chris Zawada (tc/weather icons). **NASA:** JPL (r). **65 NASA:** ESA / J. Clarke (Boston University) / Z. Levay (STScI) (6/cb); JPL (4/tc). **Science Photo Library:** California Association for Research in Astronomy (5/ca). **66 iStockphoto.com:** Cheryl Savala (l/light bulbs on red frame) (br/Jupiter's rings) (tr/Uranus's rings); JPL / University of Arizona (ca/Jupiter). **NASA:** JPL (cb/Neptune). **Science Photo Library:** California Association for Research in Astronomy (c/Uranus). **66–67 Dreamstime.com:** Nikhil Gangavane (color rings). **iStockphoto.com:** Timothy Hughes (background in frame). **67 Don Dixon/www.cosmographica. com:** (bc/ring particles). **NASA:** Hubble Heritage Team (STScI / AURA) / R. G. French (Wellesley College), J. Cuzzi (NASA / Ames), L. Dones (SwRI) & J. Lissauer (NASA / Ames) (tl/Saturn's rings) (tr/large Saturn); JPL (bl/Neptune's rings); JPL / Space Science Institute (br/Shepherd moons). **68 iStockphoto.com:** Jon Larson (bl/box); Alex Slobodkin (br/ box). **NASA:** ESA / A. Feild (STScI) (3/crb/Makemake). **Science Photo Library:** Lynette Cook (3/crb/Makemake); Friedrich Saurer (2/bl). **68–69 Getty Images:** David Seed Photography (background). **69 Corbis:** Bettman (5/ca). **Dreamstime.com:** Franku (br/paper rolls). **iStockphoto.com:** (ca/picture frame) (r); Alex Slobodkin (bc/box). **Science Photo Library:** Friedrich Saurer (4/cla). **70 ESA:** DLR / FU Berlin (G. Neukum) (2/cb). **NASA:** (5/crb) (bc/Deimos); JPL (3/cra) (4/cr); JPL / Ames Research Center (6/br). **Science Photo Library:** Russell Croman (1/clb). **70–71 iStockphoto.com:** Alex Mills (wood frame). **71 Getty Images:** NASA / Time Life Pictures (9/cb). **NASA:** (11/br) (bc/Miranda) (clb/Oberon) (cla/Iapetus) (clb/ Enceladus) (clb/Rhea) (clb/Tethys) (clb/Dione); JPL / Space Science Institute (bl/Mimas); JPL-Caltech (clb/Ariel) (7/ clb) (8/cb); JPL / USGS (10/crb). **72 European Southern Observatory (ESO) :** Sebastian Deiries (6/tr). **Galaxy Picture Library:** Robin Scagell (2/clb) (2/clb) (2/tl); Michael Stecker (2/ fbl) (1/ftll). **NASA:** JPL-Caltech (1/fcla); Dr. H. A. Weaver & Mr. T. E. Smith (STScI) (7/br). **Science Photo Library:** Harvard College Observatory (3/bl); Rev. Ronald Royer (4/bc); John Thomas (5/crb). **73 Getty Images:** Steve Bonini (1). **74 The Natural History Museum, London:** (cl). **Science Photo Library:** Manfred Kage (fcra) (cb/iron meteorite); Detlev Van Ravenswaay (crb). **74–75 NASA:** Image courtesy of Earth Sciences & Image Analysis Laboratory, NASA Johnson Space Center, "The Gateway to Astronaut Photography of Earth" (http://eol.jsc.nasa.gov, photo no. ISS007-E-10807) (b). **75 Alamy Images:** Images of Africa Photobank (tl). **Simon Collins:** (clb). **Corbis:** Tony Hallas / Science Faction (cra). **NASA:** Johnson Space Center (fcla). **The Natural History Museum, London:** (cr/Nakhla meteorite). **Science Photo Library:** Detlev Van Ravenswaay (crb). **76–77 NASA. 78 iStockphoto.com:** Marco Malavasi (bl/microphone pane); Nick Schlax (ftl/meter). **NASA:** Compton Gamma Ray Observatory (bl/gamma rays); CXC / ASU / J. Hester et al. (br/x-ray); G. Hennessy (USNO) et al. / UIT (br/ultraviolet). **78–79 iStockphoto.com:** Cristian Nitu (background / main image). **79 iStockphoto.com:** Mark Evans (br/green and red power lights). **NASA:** ESA / JPL / Arizona State University (fbl/visible light); JPL-Caltech / R. Gehrz (University of Minnesota) (bl/ infrared). **Science Photo Library:** NRAO / AUI / NSF (c/radio waves). **80 Corbis:** Bettman (2/crb). **Getty Images:** (3/cr); Hulton Archive (1/br); Steve Liss / Time & Life Pictures (4/cra); William Franklin / Time Life Pictures (5/cra); New York Times Co. (6/tr). **80–81 iStockphoto.com:** Teun van den Dries (background). **81 Corbis:** Jonathan Blair (10/tc); Roger Ressmeyer (7/bc). **Getty Images:** Associated Press, Inc. (9/cla). **Science Photo Library:** John Irwin Collection / American Institute Of Physics (8/clb). **82 Corbis:** Mike Hutchings / Reuters (3/cr) (2/fcra); Roger Ressmeyer (4/fcrb).

82–83 Corbis: Roger Ressmeyer (1/main image). **iStockphoto.com:** (c/camera lens). **83 Corbis:** Roger Ressmeyer (6/cl). **Getty Images:** Joe McNally (5/fcla); STR / AFP (7/fclb). **84 Corbis:** Jim Sugar (1/clb). **Getty Images:** Paco Elvira / Cover (2/cb). **84–85 Corbis:** (private jet background). **Getty Images:** Joe McNally (3/cb). **85 Getty Images:** Torsten Blackwood / AFP (5/fcrb). **Science Photo Library:** John Sanford (4/cb). **86 Getty Images:** Stocktrek Images (cl/payload). **iStockphoto.com:** Frank van den Bergh (l/grass). **NASA:** (l/ rocket stages). **86–87 Getty Images:** CSA Plastoc (tl/toy rocket). **Dreamstime.com:** Stacey Newman (grass background, 3/4 to right). **87 Dreamstime.com:** Feng Yu (r/ringbinder). **iStockphoto.com:** (tc/burning cable). **NASA:** JPL (bl/ion drive). **Science Photo Library:** RIA Novosti (cra/launch pad). **88 Corbis:** Erik Simonsen / Photographer's Choice (cb/Envisat). **Science Photo Library:** European Space Agency (fcr/space junk); NASA (ca/CloudSat). **88–89 Getty Images:** Greg Dale / National Geographic (main observatory image). **89 Science Photo Library:** David Ducros (clb/telecommunications); Friedrich Saurer (cra/navigation satellite). **90 ESA:** PACS Consortium (tr/Whirlpool Galaxy). **iStockphoto.com:** (bc/masking tape). **90–91 iStockphoto.com:** Nicholas Belton (blueprint background); Terry Wilson (page curls). **91 Getty Images:** NASA / ESA / STScI / M. Robberto, HST Orion Treasury Team / Science Photo Library (cr) (fcra/paper clip). **iStockphoto.com:** (fcrb/masking tape). **NASA:** STScI (br); UMass / D. Wang et al. (tr). **92 ESA:** C. Carreau (cb/Rosetta). **iStockphoto.com:** Bakaleev Aleksey (cb/picture frame); Gillian Mowbray (bl/books). **NASA:** JPL-Caltech (fcr/Voyager). **92–93 ESA:** NASA (ca/Cassini and Huygens). **iStockphoto.com:** Wendell Franks (ca/box); Oleg Prikhodko (shelves background). **93 ESA:** JPL (cra/Mars Express). **iStockphoto.com:** Stephen Jaffe / AFP (cla/NEAR Shoemaker) (br/blue box). **iStockphoto.com:** (clb/book spine); Matteo Rinaldi (cra/triangle tag); Terry Wilson (bc/curl on sticker); JPL-Caltech (fcrb/Stardust). **NASA:** JPL (bl/Galileo). **94 Corbis:** NASA / EPA (2/cra). **Getty Images:** NASA - JPL / Stewart Cook - Online USA, Inc. / Hulton Archive (1/bl). **94–95 NASA:** JPL (5/background). **95 Corbis:** NASA / JPL (3/bc); NASA / Science Faction / Encyclopedia (4/ca). **96 Corbis:** Bettmann (cra/sending messages). **NASA:** JPL (cl/ planet hunting). **Science Photo Library:** Dr Seth Shostak (cl/listening for signs); U.S. Geological Survey (tc/planet). **96–97 NASA:** ESA / G. Bacon (STScI) (starry background). **97 The Advertising Archives:** (tr/fictional aliens). **Getty Images:** Dr David Phillips / Visuals Unlimited (tl/br faces). **NASA:** ESA / G. Bacon (STScI) (br/exoplanet); JPL (cra/looking on Mars); USGS (clb/Eath). **98 NASA:** JPL (Juno). **98–99 Dreamstime.com:** Peter Soderstrom (background). **ESA:** Medialab (Milky Way background) **99 ESA:** C. Carreau (clb/ Gaia). **Getty Images:** NASA / Stocktrek RF (tr/Curiosity). **iStockphoto.com:** (stamp shapes). **NASA:** (crb/James Webb); JPL (tl/GRAIL). **100–101 NASA. 102 Corbis:** Lebrecht Music & Arts (1/tr). **NASA:** Johnson Space Center / Bettmann (br). **103 Corbis:** NASA / Xinhua Photo / Sygma (7/cl). **Getty Images:** Robert Laberge (8/ca). **NASA:** (4/tl) (5/cl) (6/crb).**104 Corbis:** NASA / Roger Ressmeyer (crb/daily life). **Dreamstime. com:** Xunbin Pan (r/car. **NASA:** (bc/daily life); Johnson Space Center (cl/space sensation). **104–105 Corbis:** NASA / Science Faction (background). **105 Corbis:** NASA / Roger Ressmeyer (tl/training); Jim Sugar (cla). **Dorling Kindersley:** Courtesy of Helen Sharman (bl). **NASA:** (cra); Marshall Space Flight Center / Science@NASA (br). **106 Alamy Images:** Interfoto (br/TV set). **Dorling Kindersley:** Courtesy of ESA (cla). **iStockphoto.com:** (br/screen image) (cra) (fcra) (ftr) (tr); Marshall Space Flight Center (bl). **106–107 iStockphoto.com:** (picture frames). **107 Corbis:** NASA (bl/Lunar Rover) (br/Lunar Module). **NASA:** (tl) (ca) (cla) (cra) (fcla) (ftl) (tc) (tr). **108 iStockphoto.com:** Alexander Dolgin (cra/mannequin head) (clb/boots) (r/spacesuit). **NASA:** (c/spacesuit). **108–109 iStockphoto.com:** Hasan Kursad Ergan (b/parquet). **Photolibrary:** Josu Altzelai / age fotostock (b/pavement and bottom of shop window). **109 iStockphoto.com:** (tl/frame) (clb/gloves) (tl/astronauts). **NASA:** (clb/shirt). **110 NASA:** (2/br). **111 Corbis:** Bettmann (3/bl); NASA / Roger Ressmeyer (4/bc). **Dreamstime. com:** Brad Calkins (tl/tweezers); Svietlanan (tr/box). **NASA:** (ftr) (5/cra) (6/crb/top) (6/fcrb/bottom). **112–113 NASA. 114–115 NASA:** (background). **115 iStockphoto.com:** (tl/ hand). **116 Corbis:** Bettmann (1/cla). **NASA:** (2/c) (3/bl). **117 grungetextures.com:** (br/handle). **NASA:** (5/cb) (6/cr) (7/bl). **118 Alamy Images:** Fackler Non CC (bl/suitcases). **iStockphoto.com:** David Gunn (bc/passport); Ben Ryan (fcla/ luggage cart); Charles Taylor (clb/passport). **NASA:** (cr/tag) (2/ fcrb); Bill Ingalls (3/cr/Greg Olsen); Kennedy Space Center (KSC) (1/tl). **118–119 Corbis:** Ron Chapple Stock (stickers on suitcase). **iStockphoto.com:** Jamie Farrant (passport stamps); Matthew Gough (main suitcase & green suitcase). **119 Alamy Images:** Nikreates (br/luggage). **Dreamstime.com:** Robert Mizerek (bc/tickets). **iStockphoto.com:** David Gunn (cr/passport); Dmitry Mordvintsev (br/magazine pages). **NASA:** (6/cla) (7/cr); Gagarin Cosmonaut Training Center (5/ cl). **courtesy Virgin Galactic:** (8/br). **120 Corbis:** Anatoly Maltsev / EPA (c/Soyuz FG); Reuters (tl/Ariane 5). **Dreamstime. com:** Eyewave (fcrb/books); Claudio Fichera (br/robot). **iStockphoto.com:** David Gunn (tl/books). **NASA:** Marshall Space Flight Center (r/Saturn V). **121 Corbis:** Jim Campbell / Areo News Network / Pool / Reuters (tr/SpaceShipOne); Li Gang / Xinhua Press (br/Long March). **Dreamstime.com:** Michael Flippo (b/ balls); Robin Kizzar (bc/ two); Moutwtrng (fcrb/toy car). **NASA:** (tl/Ares 1); Marshall Space Flight Center (clb/Space Shuttle). **122 NASA:** (1/tc) (2/br). **122–123 Alamy Images:** Directphoto.org (street scene background). **123 ESA:** S. Corvaja (4/tc). **NASA:** Pat Rawlings (SAIC) (3/tl). **Science Photo Library:** Bigelow Aerospace (5/tr). **126–128 CNES, ESA, European Southern Observatory (ESO) & NASA.**

Jacket images: *Front:* CNES, ESA, European Southern Observatory (ESO) & NASA. *Back:* CNES, ESA, European Southern Observatory (ESO) & NASA.

All other images © Dorling Kindersley
For further information see:
www.dkimages.com